FAISAL

FAISAL

Rebecca Stefoff

FONS VITAE

Published in 2007 by
Fons Vitae
49 Mockingbird Valley Drive
Louisville, KY 40207
http://www.fonsvitae.com
Email: fonsvitaeky@aol.com

Library of Congress Control Number: 2007937222

ISBN 1-891785-10-9

Contents

WORLD LEADERS PAST & PRESENT

John Adams
John Quincy Adams
Konrad Adenauer
Alexander the Great
Salvador Allende
Marc Antony
Corazon Aquino
Yasir Arafat
King Arthur
Hafez al-Assad
Kemal Atatürk
Attila
Clement Attlee
Augustus Caesar
Menachem Begin
David Ben-Gurion
Otto von Bismarck
Léon Blum
Simon Bolívar
Cesare Borgia
Willy Brandt
Leonid Brezhnev
Julius Caesar
John Calvin
Jimmy Carter
Fidel Castro
Catherine the Great
Charlemagne
Chiang Kai-Shek
Winston Churchill
Georges Clemenceau
Cleopatra
Constantine the Great
Hernán Cortés
Oliver Cromwell
Georges-Jacques Danton
Jefferson Davis
Moshe Dayan
Charles de Gaulle
Eamon De Valera
Eugene Debs
Deng Xiaoping
Benjamin Disraeli
Alexander Dubček
François & Jean-Claude Duvalier
Dwight Eisenhower
Eleanor of Aquitaine
Elizabeth I
Faisal
Ferdinand & Isabella
Francisco Franco
Benjamin Franklin
Frederick the Great
Indira Gandhi
Mohandas Gandhi
Giuseppe Garibaldi
Amin & Bashir Gemayel
Genghis Khan
William Gladstone
Mikhail Gorbachev
Ulysses S. Grant
Ernesto "Che" Guevara
Tenzin Gyatso
Alexander Hamilton
Dag Hammarskjöld
Henry VIII
Henry of Navarre
Paul von Hindenburg
Hirohito
Adolf Hitler
Ho Chi Minh
King Hussein
Ivan the Terrible
Andrew Jackson
James I
Wojciech Jaruzelski
Thomas Jefferson
Joan of Arc
Pope John XXIII
Pope John Paul II
Lyndon Johnson
Benito Juárez
John Kennedy
Robert Kennedy
Jomo Kenyatta
Ayatollah Khomeini
Nikita Khrushchev
Kim Il Sung
Martin Luther King, Jr.
Henry Kissinger
Kublai Khan
Lafayette
Robert E. Lee
Vladimir Lenin
Abraham Lincoln
David Lloyd George
Louis XIV
Martin Luther
Judas Maccabeus
James Madison
Nelson & Winnie Mandela
Mao Zedong
Ferdinand Marcos
George Marshall
Mary, Queen of Scots
Tomáš Masaryk
Golda Meir
Klemens von Metternich
James Monroe
Hosni Mubarak
Robert Mugabe
Benito Mussolini
Napoléon Bonaparte
Gamal Abdel Nasser
Jawaharlal Nehru
Nero
Nicholas II
Richard Nixon
Kwame Nkrumah
Daniel Ortega
Mohammed Reza Pahlavi
Thomas Paine
Charles Stewart Parnell
Pericles
Juan Perón
Peter the Great
Pol Pot
Muammar el-Qaddafi
Ronald Reagan
Cardinal Richelieu
Maximilien Robespierre
Eleanor Roosevelt
Franklin Roosevelt
Theodore Roosevelt
Anwar Sadat
Haile Selassie
Prince Sihanouk
Jan Smuts
Joseph Stalin
Sukarno
Sun Yat-sen
Tamerlane
Mother Teresa
Margaret Thatcher
Josip Broz Tito
Toussaint L'Ouverture
Leon Trotsky
Pierre Trudeau
Harry Truman
Queen Victoria
Lech Walesa
George Washington
Chaim Weizmann
Woodrow Wilson
Xerxes
Emiliano Zapata
Zhou Enlai

CHELSEA HOUSE PUBLISHERS

ON LEADERSHIP

Arthur M. Schlesinger, jr.

LEADERSHIP, it may be said, is really what makes the world go round. Love no doubt smooths the passage; but love is a private transaction between consenting adults. Leadership is a public transaction with history. The idea of leadership affirms the capacity of individuals to move, inspire, and mobilize masses of people so that they act together in pursuit of an end. Sometimes leadership serves good purposes, sometimes bad; but whether the end is benign or evil, great leaders are those men and women who leave their personal stamp on history.

Now, the very concept of leadership implies the proposition that individuals can make a difference. This proposition has never been universally accepted. From classical times to the present day, eminent thinkers have regarded individuals as no more than the agents and pawns of larger forces, whether the gods and goddesses of the ancient world or, in the modern era, race, class, nation, the dialectic, the will of the people, the spirit of the times, history itself. Against such forces, the individual dwindles into insignificance.

So contends the thesis of historical determinism. Tolstoy's great novel *War and Peace* offers a famous statement of the case. Why, Tolstoy asked, did millions of men in the Napoleonic Wars, denying their human feelings and their common sense, move back and forth across Europe slaughtering their fellows? "The war," Tolstoy answered, "was bound to happen simply because it was bound to happen." All prior history predetermined it. As for leaders, they, Tolstoy said, "are but the labels that serve to give a name to an end and, like labels, they have the least possible connection with the event." The greater the leader, "the more conspicuous the inevitability and the predestination of every act he commits." The leader, said Tolstoy, is "the slave of history."

Determinism takes many forms. Marxism is the determinism of class. Nazism the determinism of race. But the idea of men and women as the slaves of history runs athwart the deepest human instincts. Rigid determinism abolishes the idea of human freedom—

the assumption of free choice that underlies every move we make, every word we speak, every thought we think. It abolishes the idea of human responsibility, since it is manifestly unfair to reward or punish people for actions that are by definition beyond their control. No one can live consistently by any deterministic creed. The Marxist states prove this themselves by their extreme susceptibility to the cult of leadership.

More than that, history refutes the idea that individuals make no difference. In December 1931 a British politician crossing Park Avenue in New York City between 76th and 77th Streets around 10:30 P.M. looked in the wrong direction and was knocked down by an automobile—a moment, he later recalled, of a man aghast, a world aglare: "I do not understand why I was not broken like an eggshell or squashed like a gooseberry." Fourteen months later an American politician, sitting in an open car in Miami, Florida, was fired on by an assassin; the man beside him was hit. Those who believe that individuals make no difference to history might well ponder whether the next two decades would have been the same had Mario Constasino's car killed Winston Churchill in 1931 and Giuseppe Zangara's bullet killed Franklin Roosevelt in 1933. Suppose, in addition, that Adolf Hitler had been killed in the street fighting during the Munich *Putsch* of 1923 and that Lenin had died of typhus during World War I. What would the 20th century be like now?

For better or for worse, individuals do make a difference. "The notion that a people can run itself and its affairs anonymously," wrote the philosopher William James, "is now well known to be the silliest of absurdities. Mankind does nothing save through initiatives on the part of inventors, great or small, and imitation by the rest of us—these are the sole factors in human progress. Individuals of genius show the way, and set the patterns, which common people then adopt and follow."

Leadership, James suggests, means leadership in thought as well as in action. In the long run, leaders in thought may well make the greater difference to the world. But, as Woodrow Wilson once said, "Those only are leaders of men, in the general eye, who lead in action. . . . It is at their hands that new thought gets its translation into the crude language of deeds." Leaders in thought often invent in solitude and obscurity, leaving to later generations the tasks of imitation. Leaders in action—the leaders portrayed in this series—have to be effective in their own time.

And they cannot be effective by themselves. They must act in response to the rhythms of their age. Their genius must be adapted, in a phrase of William James's, "to the receptivities of the moment." Leaders are useless without followers. "There goes the mob," said the French politician hearing a clamor in the streets. "I am their leader. I must follow them." Great leaders turn the inchoate emotions of the mob to purposes of their own. They seize on the opportunities of their time, the hopes, fears, frustrations, crises, potentialities. They succeed when events have prepared the way for them, when the community is awaiting to be aroused, when they can provide the clarifying and organizing ideas. Leadership ignites the circuit between the individual and the mass and thereby alters history.

It may alter history for better or for worse. Leaders have been responsible for the most extravagant follies and most monstrous crimes that have beset suffering humanity. They have also been vital in such gains as humanity has made in individual freedom, religious and racial tolerance, social justice, and respect for human rights.

There is no sure way to tell in advance who is going to lead for good and who for evil. But a glance at the gallery of men and women in *World Leaders—Past and Present* suggests some useful tests.

One test is this: Do leaders lead by force or by persuasion? By command or by consent? Through most of history leadership was exercised by the divine right of authority. The duty of followers was to defer and to obey. "Theirs not to reason why / Theirs but to do and die." On occasion, as with the so-called enlightened despots of the 18th century in Europe, absolutist leadership was animated by humane purposes. More often, absolutism nourished the passion for domination, land, gold, and conquest and resulted in tyranny.

The great revolution of modern times has been the revolution of equality. The idea that all people should be equal in their legal condition has undermined the old structure of authority, hierarchy, and deference. The revolution of equality has had two contrary effects on the nature of leadership. For equality, as Alexis de Tocqueville pointed out in his great study *Democracy in America*, might mean equality in servitude as well as equality in freedom.

"I know of only two methods of establishing equality in the political world," Tocqueville wrote. "Rights must be given to every citizen, or none at all to anyone . . . save one, who is the master of all." There was no middle ground "between the sovereignty of all and the absolute power of one man." In his astonishing prediction of 20th-century totalitarian dictatorship, Tocqueville explained how the revolution of equality could lead to the *"Führerprinzip"* and more terrible absolutism than the world had ever known.

But when rights are given to every citizen and the sovereignty of all is established, the problem of leadership takes a new form, becomes more exacting than ever before. It is easy to issue commands and enforce them by the rope and the stake, the concentration camp and the *gulag.* It is much harder to use argument and achievement to overcome opposition and win consent. The Founding Fathers of the United States understood the difficulty. They believed that history had given them the opportunity to decide, as Alexander Hamilton wrote in the first Federalist Paper, whether men are indeed capable of basing government on "reflection and choice, or whether they are forever destined to depend . . . on accident and force."

Government by reflection and choice called for a new style of leadership and a new quality of followership. It required leaders to be responsive to popular concerns, and it required followers to be active and informed participants in the process. Democracy does not eliminate emotion from politics; sometimes it fosters demagoguery; but it is confident that, as the greatest of democratic leaders put it, you cannot fool all of the people all of the time. It measures leadership by results and retires those who overreach or falter or fail.

It is true that in the long run despots are measured by results too. But they can postpone the day of judgment, sometimes indefinitely, and in the meantime they can do infinite harm. It is also true that democracy is no guarantee of virtue and intelligence in government, for the voice of the people is not necessarily the voice of God. But democracy, by assuring the right of opposition, offers built-in resistance to the evils inherent in absolutism. As the theologian Reinhold Niebuhr summed it up, "Man's capacity for justice makes democracy possible, but man's inclination to injustice makes democracy necessary."

A second test for leadership is the end for which power is sought. When leaders have as their goal the supremacy of a master race or the promotion of totalitarian revolution or the acquisition and exploitation of colonies or the protection of greed and privilege or the preservation of personal power, it is likely that their leadership will do little to advance the cause of humanity. When their goal is the abolition of slavery, the liberation of women, the enlargement of opportunity for the poor and powerless, the extension of equal rights to racial minorities, the defense of the freedoms of expression and opposition, it is likely that their leadership will increase the sum of human liberty and welfare.

Leaders have done great harm to the world. They have also conferred great benefits. You will find both sorts in this series. Even "good" leaders must be regarded with a certain wariness. Leaders are not demigods; they put on their trousers one leg after another just like ordinary mortals. No leader is infallible, and every leader needs to be reminded of this at regular intervals. Irreverence irritates leaders but is their salvation. Unquestioning submission corrupts leaders and demeans followers. Making a cult of a leader is always a mistake. Fortunately hero worship generates its own antidote. "Every hero," said Emerson, "becomes a bore at last."

The signal benefit the great leaders confer is to embolden the rest of us to live according to our own best selves, to be active, insistent, and resolute in affirming our own sense of things. For great leaders attest to the reality of human freedom against the supposed inevitabilities of history. And they attest to the wisdom and power that may lie within the most unlikely of us, which is why Abraham Lincoln remains the supreme example of great leadership. A great leader, said Emerson, exhibits new possibilities to all humanity. "We feed on genius. . . . Great men exist that there may be greater men."

Great leaders, in short, justify themselves by emancipating and empowering their followers. So humanity struggles to master its destiny, remembering with Alexis de Tocqueville: "It is true that around every man a fatal circle is traced beyond which he cannot pass; but within the wide verge of that circle he is powerful and free; as it is with man, so with communities."

1

The Oil Weapon

America's complete support of Zionism against the Arabs makes it extremely difficult for us to continue to supply U.S. petroleum needs and even to maintain friendly relations with America.
—KING FAISAL
July 1973

In October 1973, a war broke out between the Arab Muslim nations of Egypt and Syria and the Jewish nation of Israel. Almost immediately, the Islamic oil-producing countries banned sales of petroleum to Israel and its supporters, including the United States. For the first time ever, the nations that owned some of the world's richest energy reserves were using petroleum as a political weapon, and the amount of oil available on the world market dropped sharply. It touched off the most severe energy crisis in world history.

The crisis hit hardest in the United States, where energy use per person was the highest in the world. Automobile owners were the first to feel the pinch. For the first time since World War II, gasoline was rationed, which meant that drivers could fuel their cars only on certain days of the month — and usually only after waiting in long lines, sometimes for hours. Some service stations set a limit on how much gas a customer could buy, and some stations had no gas to sell at all.

An oil rig in the desert of Saudi Arabia. One-quarter of the earth's known oil deposits lie beneath the sands of the Middle Eastern kingdom, making it one of the wealthiest and most economically powerful nations in the world.

Faysal ibn 'Abd al-Aziz, king of Saudi Arabia from 1964 until 1975. King Faisal, as he was known in the West, fostered close relations between his nation and the United States — until 1973, when he halted oil exports to the United States to protest that nation's alliance with Israel.

Soon people began to conserve energy and to question how it was being spent. The dazzling display of neon in New York City's Times Square went dark. Each night television newscasters reminded viewers that the White House thermostat had been turned down to an energy-saving 68 degrees Fahrenheit. As autumn gave way to winter and shortages of heating oil, Americans wondered how long the crisis would last. Still, few realized that the days of unlimited, inexpensive energy were gone for good.

The ban, or embargo, on petroleum sales was accompanied by the most rapid acquisition of wealth ever experienced by developing nations. In addition to halting sales to Israel's supporters, the oil-producing countries raised the price of the oil they sold to other nations. The cost of a barrel of crude oil, which had remained almost unchanged for several decades, quadrupled within 10 weeks and continued to rise steeply for a long time thereafter.

The effects of rising oil prices were felt around the world as the costs of energy and of all the products made with energy skyrocketed. Countries that did not have petroleum were forced to pay high prices or do without, while countries that had it suddenly became rich beyond imagining — and the richest of these was Saudi Arabia, whose income from oil soon exceeded $100 million a day.

The events of October 1973 forever changed the world's pattern of wealth and energy consumption. The Arab nations of the Middle East, for centuries little more than pawns in the international political maneuverings of such world powers as Great Britain, France, Turkey, Germany, the Soviet Union, and the United States, had suddenly turned the tables and were calling the shots themselves. "Petropower" was the Western media's name for the phenomenon. And as Saudi Arabia and the other oil-producing nations prospered, another term was born: *petrodollars*.

Motorists wait in line for gasoline at a Los Angeles service station during the 1973 Arab oil embargo. The oil shortages in the United States, Canada, Europe, and Japan that resulted from the Saudi embargo and oil price hikes brought about the worst energy crisis the industrialized countries had experienced since World War II.

The forces that led to the oil embargo and the new Arab wealth are complex; they span centuries and continents, geology and history, religion and politics. But they came together in the remarkable individual who was the leading force behind the oil embargo, the world energy crisis, and the newfound political power of the Muslim nations of the Middle East: King Faisal of Saudi Arabia.

The 68-year-old Saudi monarch had long been at the center of events in the region. In 1948, when the state of Israel was created with the approval of the United Nations — and over the opposition of the Muslim countries, which held that the Arabs living within the boundaries of the new nation were being deprived of their homeland — six Arab nations attacked Israel. One of them was Saudi Arabia, then ruled by Faisal's father, King Ibn Sa'ūd. The Israelis won the 1948 war, and they won again in 1956 when, with British and French assistance, they invaded Egypt. In 1967 Israel defeated Egypt, Jordan, and Syria, conquering territory from each country, including all of the holy city of Jerusalem. As in 1956, the Saudis provided large amounts of monetary aid to the Arab nations waging war against the Israelis, but to no avail.

Israeli troops launch a mortar attack on Syrian positions during the October War of 1973, which pitted Israel against its Arab neighbors, Syria and Egypt. In support of the two Arab nations, Faisal led Saudi Arabia and other oil-producing Muslim nations in banning oil sales to the United States, Israel's closest ally.

By 1973, the Arab nations of the Middle East had already gone to war against Israel three times — with a humiliating lack of success. Saudi Arabia is the birthplace of Islam and the spiritual center of the Arab and Muslim worlds, and as its king, Faisal shared the feelings of Muslims everywhere that Jerusalem should remain a Muslim city. He also believed, like nearly all Arabs at the time, that Palestine had been unfairly taken away from its rightful owners and that the state of Israel had no right to exist. When Egypt and Syria attacked Israel on October 6, 1973, he supported them financially, as his nation had done in the past. But it was against the United States that he struck the Arabs' strongest blow—the oil embargo.

Faisal was angry at the United States for several reasons. Before he had become king in 1964, Faisal had been his country's foreign minister and ambassador to the United Nations for years, and he felt that the Americans had not always acted in good faith toward the Arabs. On several occasions he had been assured by American diplomats that the United States would treat Arab claims fairly, but he believed that the U.S. had not lived up to these commitments. Furthermore, Faisal agreed with many Arabs that the American oil companies had made huge fortunes from their operations in Arab oil fields and that it was time for the Arabs to take full control of these valuable resources.

These were the underlying factors, but it was a specific event that caused Faisal to issue the oil embargo that shook the world. Soon after the October War started, Faisal's minister of state returned from Washington, D.C., bearing U.S. president Richard Nixon's assurance that the United States would seek a "peaceful, just, and honorable" settlement to the Arab-Israeli conflict and to the problem of thousands of Palestinian Arab refugees displaced by Israel's conquests. After announcing this at a press conference, the minister then informed Faisal that Nixon understood the Arabs' concerns and shared them, and that U.S. aid to Israel would not be increased. But the very next day, Nixon asked the U.S. Congress to authorize emergency aid to Israel in the colossal sum of $2.2 billion.

Muslim pilgrims at the Kaaba in the court of the Grand Mosque at Mecca, Saudi Arabia. Muslims believe that the Kaaba contains a black stone given to the biblical patriarch Abraham by the archangel Gabriel. Muslims throughout the world turn to face this stone, considered the most sacred object in Islam, during their prayers.

One day after the news of Nixon's aid request broke in Riyadh, the capital of Saudi Arabia, Faisal announced the oil embargo. The Saudi king regarded it as a *jihad*, or Muslim holy war. It was to be fought not on battlefields but rather in oil refineries, corporate boardrooms, and across negotiating tables.

The Arabs failed to win on the battlefield in October 1973. The embargo, too, ran out of steam after five months. Nevertheless, Faisal had changed the world in fundamental ways. He had made the Western nations acknowledge the power of petroleum politics. He had brought the often-warring Arab nations together in unity — but he had also damaged the image of Arabs held by Westerners and the relationship between his country and the United States. In a single act, Faisal emerged as one of the world's most important leaders.

The 1300-year-old Dome of the Rock in Jerusalem, which Muslims believe rests on the site where Muhammad, the founder of Islam, ascended to heaven. Muslims consider Jerusalem the third holiest city, after Mecca and Medina in Saudi Arabia. Jerusalem was captured from the Arab country of Jordan by Israel in the Six-Day War of 1967.

Faisal may have emerged as a world leader of great importance seemingly overnight, but at home in Saudi Arabia he had been a leader for more than 50 years. Although he ruled as king of Saudi Arabia for less than a dozen years, from 1964 to his death in 1975, he had served as foreign minister, ambassador, and chief link between his nation and the world since 1919. A son of Saudi Arabia's founder, Faisal had become the first of his royal clan to visit nations outside the Arabian Peninsula, and he had been on hand when oil was discovered beneath his nation's desert sands. As king, he planned the rapid modernization of what had become one of the richest — yet one of the most traditional — countries in the world. Deeply committed to Islam, Faisal sought to make his nation a powerful and respected force in world politics without compromising its age-old traditions. It was something he believed in right from the start, when he was a child in the colorful, extravagant, and proud royal house of Sa'ūd.

King Faisal with U.S. president Richard Nixon during one of Faisal's many visits to Washington, D.C., in the early 1970s. Despite the 1973 oil embargo, which occurred while Nixon was in office, the United States maintained close relations with Saudi Arabia in subsequent years.

2

Islam and the House of Sa'ūd

> ***How often have the few conquered the many through the will of Allah.***
> —the Koran

The huge, wedge-shaped Arabian Peninsula is separated from Egypt and the rest of Africa by the Red Sea on the west, from India by the Persian Gulf on the east, and is bordered on the north by Iraq and Jordan. South of the peninsula is the Arabian Sea, part of the Indian Ocean. There are a number of small countries along its eastern and southern coasts, but Saudi Arabia, the third-largest country in Asia, occupies more than 80 percent of the entire peninsula.

People have lived in Arabia for thousands of years, but for much of that time the peninsula has been largely unknown to the rest of the world. Harsh deserts and warlike tribespeople long kept outsiders from venturing far into its interior. And although the tribes and small states along the coasts engaged in trade with other peoples, they usually did so by venturing forth with their goods in camel caravans or swift sailing vessels; traders from other countries were seldom welcome in Arabia.

Dressed in traditional veils and long robes, Muslim women walk along a corridor leading to the tomb of Muhammad at the Prophet's Mosque in Medina. The Saudi cities of Mecca and Medina have been the object of pilgrimages by devout Muslims for centuries.

Although for many centuries the Roman Empire included a province known as Arabia, that province actually consisted of the present-day nation of Jordan, with Egypt's Sinai peninsula and a bit of northernmost Saudi Arabia thrown in. The Romans were unable to extend their rule into the heart of Arabia; an invasion in 24 B.C. failed, leaving the Roman legionaries and their commander, Aelius Gallus, to perish miserably in the desert. The greater part of Arabia remained an unknown and unvisited mystery. It was populated by roving tribes of camel-herding nomads and farmers who settled in small communities at the rare oases, fertile areas around springs or wells. The nomads, called *bedouin*, were fierce fighters who warred constantly among themselves and against the settled townspeople. By the 7th century, Arabia was a patchwork of city-states and tribal confederations, ruled by many rival *emirs*, or princes. Some of its people were Jews or Christians, but most were spirit worshipers with no formal religion.

A portion of the Nejd region in north-central Saudi Arabia. The country's interior is made up of arid desert lands where summer temperatures often reach 120 degrees Fahrenheit and the average annual rainfall is less than 4 inches. Along the Red Sea coast there is more rain, although temperatures are nearly as high as in the interior.

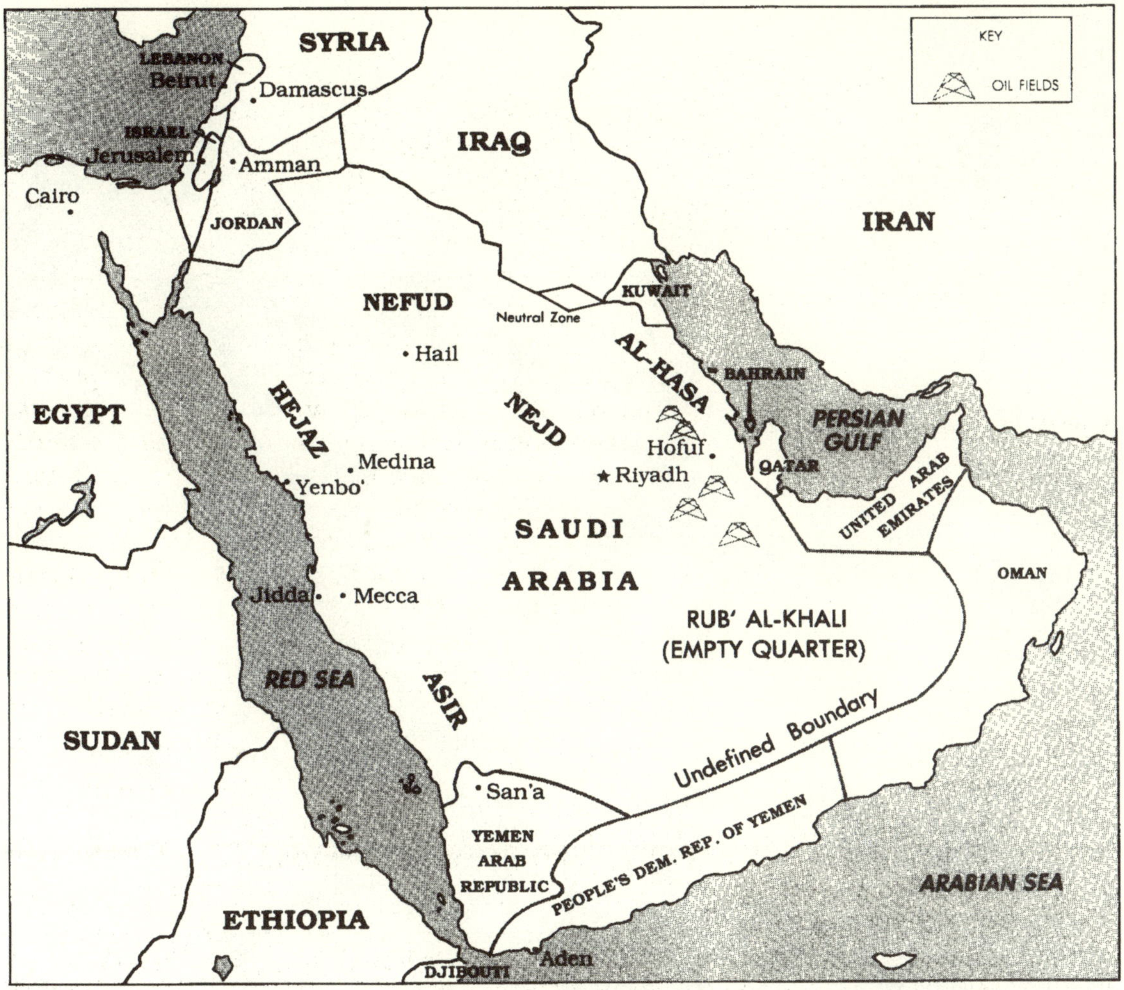

Occupying most of the Arabian Peninsula, Saudi Arabia is the birthplace of the Arab culture, which spread across the Middle East and North Africa in the Middle Ages. Today, 9 million people live in Saudi Arabia—a land about one-third the size of the continental United States—making it one of the world's most sparsely populated nations.

During the 7th century, however, the politics and religion of Arabia were changed forever. The prophet Muhammad, who would become the founder of the new faith called Islam, was born in A.D. 570 in the Arabian city of Mecca. A member of the Quraysh tribe, by the age of 25 Muhammad was working as a caravan merchant traveling between Mecca and Syria. Around the year 610 he experienced a series of religious revelations and returned to Mecca to exhort its inhabitants to abandon the worship of various gods and turn to the worship of Allah, the one God. Muhammad had little success in Mecca and in 622 went to Medina, where he was hailed as the messenger of Allah. In 630 he led an army that conquered Mecca for Islam. By the time of his death two years later, both cities had converted to the new faith.

A 16th-century Persian depiction of the prophet Muhammad ascending to heaven; such depictions of the human form are rare in Islamic art. Muhammad went to Mecca in A.D. 610 to convert the city's inhabitants from spirit worship to belief in Allah, or God. Expelled from Mecca in 622, he conquered and converted the city eight years later.

Muhammad formulated Islam (from a word meaning the surrender of oneself to the will of Allah) in part from the teachings of Judaism and Christianity, the two monotheistic religions that preceded it. Muslims believe that Allah is an all-seeing, all-powerful god and that he will reward those who perform good deeds and lead a pious life with an eternity in paradise.

Islam's emphasis on brotherhood found a receptive audience among the constantly warring tribes of Arabia, and after Muhammad's death the religion took hold throughout the peninsula. Soon the whole of Arabia was united under the rule of the *caliphs*, the spiritual leaders who succeeded Muhammad. For the first time in history, all of the Arabian tribes were under one rule and one faith. Unable to continue warring against their fellow Muslims, the fighting bedouin burst the bounds of Arabia and carried their jihad across North Africa and the Middle East.

The Arabs spread their language, culture, and faith to many parts of the Mediterranean world, and Arab civilization flowered for many centuries. Ironically, however, Arabia itself soon lost its importance as the territories it conquered grew more powerful than the conqueror. Although Muslims from every country came to Arabia to make pilgrimages to the holy cities of Mecca and Medina, as required by their faith, the Arabs who had settled in more fertile or prosperous countries had little use for their ancient homeland. Arabia became a distant province of the Muslim empires of Syria, Persia, Egypt, and Turkey. Its tribes resumed their age-old life of warfare, banditry, and the struggle for survival in a cruel land. The only people who could travel unmolested there were Muslims on pilgrimage, and they were safe only in the western coastal region called Hejaz, which contained Mecca and Medina and their seaport, Jidda.

For centuries the Ottoman Sultans had been recognized as caliphs, the successors of the prophet Mohammed and the spiritual leaders of Islam.

—MOHAMMED ALMANA
Ibn Saud biographer

For a thousand years or so, Arabia played no part in the affairs of the world and was almost forgotten by everyone outside its borders. But eventually Arabia was touched by the great age of exploration that began in Europe with Columbus's voyages to the New World. In the 17th century, a few wandering merchants and shipwrecked sailors published accounts of their travels in Arabia. These tales whetted the curiosity of explorers, who began visiting Arabia in larger numbers in the 18th century. One of these was a German named Carsten Niebuhr, the sole survivor of a Danish expedition in the 1760s. His writings give the first reliable account of the origin of modern Saudi Arabia.

After Muhammad's death in 632, Arab warriors swept across the Middle East and North Africa; within 300 years, Muslim rulers reigned from India to Spain. This painting by the 19th-century German artist Adolf Schreyer reflects Western fascination with the nomadic tribal cultures of the Arabian Peninsula.

Niebuhr reported that the tribes of the interior were excited about a new religious brotherhood called Wahhabism. Wahhabism had originated in north-central Arabia, in the region known as Nejd, and it found its strongest political ally in a *sheik*, or tribal leader, named Muhammad ibn Sa'ūd — the direct ancestor, seven generations removed, of King Faisal.

The Wahhabis, as members of the brotherhood were called, were led by Muhammad ibn 'Abd al-Wahhāb. Believing that many of the Muslims of Arabia had fallen away from pure Islam, ibn 'Abd al-Wahhāb called for a return to the strict religious behavior that had been commanded by Muhammad. He wanted the people of Nejd, or the Nejdis, to halt such practices as worshiping the shrines and tombs of holy men because these practices were not mentioned in the Koran, the holy book of Islam.

Ibn 'Abd al-Wahhāb attracted many followers. They trimmed their mustaches short, cut the hems of their long robes raggedly above the knee, and forbade the wearing of silk or fine cotton — all in an attempt to avoid the sins of luxury and vanity. But other Nejdis resented the Wahhabis' strictness, and soon ibn 'Abd al-Wahhāb was driven away from his home to wander in the desert. At this time, around 1744, he was befriended by Muhammad ibn Sa'ūd, the sheik of the village of Dariyah, a few miles north of present-day Riyadh. Ibn Sa'ūd invited ibn 'Abd al-Wahhāb to become the village's *qadi*, or holy man. The Wahhabis merged with the Saudis, or members of ibn Sa'ūd's clan, and thus was forged the alliance that was to make Wahhabism by far the most widely practiced form of Islam on the peninsula. The alliance would also make today's Saudi royal family the most powerful in Arabia.

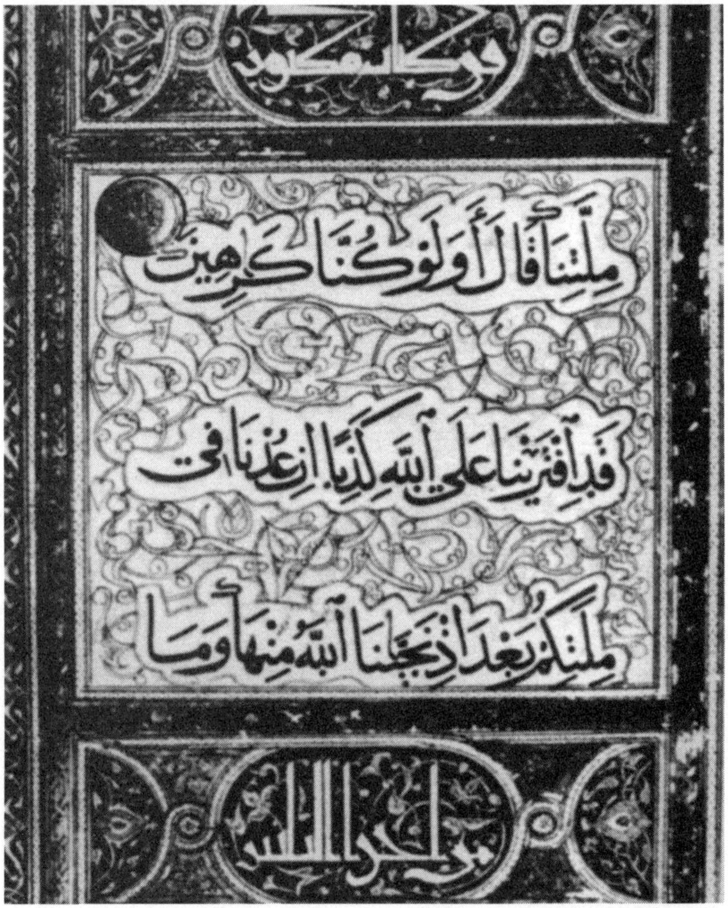

A page from a 13th-century Koran, Islam's holy book, believed by Muslims to contain the words of Allah as dictated to Muhammad by the archangel Gabriel. Saudi society and law are governed in strict accordance with the rules set forth in the Koran.

Under the leadership of the Saudis, the Wahhabis became a disciplined fighting force. Through battle and alliance, they imposed their stern version of Islam on all of the tribes of Nejd, as well as on the region called al-Hasa, on the Persian Gulf coast. In 1802, the Saudis and the Wahhabis marched on Hejaz, and by 1804, the holy cities of Mecca and Medina were controlled by Saud ibn Sa'ūd, grandson of the sheik who had given the first Wahhabis shelter at Dariyah. For the first time since the days of the Prophet Muhammad, much of Arabia was united under a single ruler.

The holy cities were a great prize. Each Muslim who wished to make a *hajj*, or pilgrimage, to the cities had to pay a pilgrim tax, along with certain other fees. These monies went to the ruler of the cities. Because the number of pilgrims each year was very great, the holy cities had become a profitable enterprise. When the upstart Wahhabis and Saudis seized this enterprise, the Ottoman Empire decided to strike back.

The Ottoman Turks were the official sovereigns of Arabia and most of the Muslim world. In practice, the Ottomans had turned over responsibility for government in Egypt and Arabia to Muhammad Ali, the Turkish viceroy, or governor, in Egypt. Muhammad Ali had ignored the internal affairs of Arabia for years; he was satisfied that all was well so long as he received the bulk of the pilgrim-tax money. Now, however, his Ottoman masters commanded him to recapture the holy cities.

Muhammad Ali mounted a fierce campaign against Hejaz, and after years of fighting, he recaptured Mecca and Medina and sent the Wahhabi and Saudi warriors fleeing into the remote deserts of Nejd. The Turks pursued, intent on teaching the Arabians a lesson. In 1819 — five years after Saud ibn Sa'ūd died and his son Abdullah ibn Sa'ūd took over as leader of the Saudi forces — the Wahhabis and Saudis finally were defeated by the Turks. Abdullah was sent to Constantinople, the Ottoman capital, where he was beheaded. Dariyah, the Saudi capital, was burned to the ground; it was never rebuilt, and today a few crumbling mud-brick walls, half covered with windblown sand, are all that remain of it.

A view of the Yemeni seaport of Mukalla in the 1950s. After the Middle Ages, such Arabian ports grew powerful as merchant centers by transporting and trading spices and slaves between Africa, Europe, India, and China. In the 17th century, coastal Arabia came under the rule of the Ottoman Empire.

An early photograph of Constantinople (now Istanbul, Turkey), capital of the Ottoman Empire, in the 1830s. In 1819, Faisal's ancestor Abdullah ibn Sa'ūd was beheaded in Constantinople after the Turks captured the independent sheikdom he ruled in Nejd. The Turks held all of Arabia until 1902.

With Hejaz firmly under their control, the Turkish forces returned to Egypt. Meanwhile, the Saudis slowly and cautiously began rebuilding a smaller state in central and eastern Nejd. Led by Turkī, they captured the city of Riyadh and made it their capital. Keeping the Wahhabi sect alive, they conquered or made alliances with many tribes and towns in central and eastern Arabia. But one powerful clan, the Rashids, wanted to rule Nejd for themselves. In 1891, they took Riyadh and drove the Saudi sheik and his family into exile.

The exiled sheik's name was 'Abd ar-Rahmān ibn Sa'ūd. He was King Faisal's grandfather. With his flight in 1891, the tumultuous modern history of Saudi Arabia begins.

'Abd ar-Rahmān was a patient and philosophical man who might have been content to live out his life in exile in the home of his friend, Sheik Mubarak of Kuwait. But he had a son of quite different mind: 'Abd al-Azīz ibn Sa'ūd, born sometime in the late 1870s. Ibn Sa'ūd — whose full name was 'Abd al-Azīz ibn 'Abd ar-Rahmān ibn Faysal ibn Turkī 'Abd Allāh ibn Muhammad Āl Sa'ūd — was determined to over-

throw the Rashids and restore his family to its place as rulers of Nejd. Ibn Sa'ūd would become the first king of Saudi Arabia. He was also Faisal's father.

Although Ibn Sa'ūd was a young boy when Riyadh fell to the Rashids, he had been brought up in the traditional Nejdi fashion and already knew how to use weapons and to train and ride horses and camels. Before going into exile in Kuwait, 'Abd ar-Rahmān's family spent several years traveling with the Bani Murra, a friendly bedouin tribe. The Bani Murra were regarded by Nejdi townspeople as the wildest and fiercest of all bedouin. From them, young Ibn Sa'ūd learned to endure hardship and privation, to travel quickly by night, to hunt and to track — skills that he would later use in war. He also acquired a profound respect for the bedouin and for their austere faith and simple traditions. Many years later, when he was king of one of the richest countries in the world, surrounded by his own harems and the palaces of his princely sons, Ibn Sa'ūd used to say that the happiest days of his life were the two harsh years he spent living in the black goat-hair tents of the bedouin.

Faisal's father, King Ibn Sa'ūd, flanked by a daughter and two aides outside his tent in the desert in 1928. In 1902, Ibn Sa'ūd captured the Nejdi city of Riyadh from its Turkish-supported governor; after 25 more years of warfare, he had united under his rule most of present-day Saudi Arabia.

The Saudi family settled in Kuwait in 1894 or 1895. Almost immediately, various members of the clan began to organize plots aimed at ousting the Rashids and regaining power. Sheik Mubarak, however, advised them to move with caution. The Rashids, he said, were favored by the Turkish overlords, who might defend them. Furthermore, Great Britain had become a power in the region, signing treaties with Mubarak and other Persian Gulf sheiks. Britain and Turkey were allies, and so the British, too, would stand behind the Rashids. Without such support, Mubarak feared, the Saudis would be unable to dislodge the Rashids — and indeed, several Saudi attacks on Rashid strongholds ended in disastrous defeats.

Ibn Sa'ūd, however, burned with impatience to restore his family to glory. In early 1902, he embarked on a daring adventure, the story of which is still recounted in the bazaars and markets of Arabia. He left Kuwait with 40 loyal followers, vowing not to return until he had captured Riyadh or died in the attempt. He was about 22 years old.

On the way to Riyadh, Ibn Sa'ūd gathered some 200 bedouin warriors. But upon reaching the outskirts of Riyadh, he was forced to admit that so small a force could never overcome the well-fortified town with its large garrison of soldiers. So he devised a cunning stratagem. With 15 close companions, he scaled the walls at night and made his way silently to the house of a family that had remained loyal to the Saudis. Once inside the house, he broke through the walls into neighboring houses, binding and gagging their owners, until he and his strike force were hidden in the house directly opposite the fort where the Rashid governor of Riyadh slept every night. Knowing that the governor left the fort every morning to visit his harem, Ibn Sa'ūd waited until the narrow door of the fort inched open. Then, with wild cries, he and his men raced into the courtyard. A fierce struggle followed, and in the confusion the governor was killed. Those in the garrison who had not been cut down surrendered, and with the surrender the townspeople proclaimed loyalty to the Saudis. Ibn Sa'ūd had recaptured Riyadh.

Other conquests soon followed. With the number of their followers growing daily as word of their success spread, the Saudis were victorious over both Rashid soldiers and the Turkish troops who arrived to restore order. The Turks withdrew in 1904, and the head of the Rashid house was killed in battle in 1906. 'Abd ar-Rahmān rewarded his son by making him the leader of the Saudi clan.

Ibn Sa'ūd was now the undisputed ruler of all Nejd. But he was not yet satisfied. He intended to reclaim the entire empire of his 18th-century ancestors and would soon continue to wage war to achieve that goal.

It was against this backdrop that Faisal was born.

3

A Widening World

King Faisal . . . came to symbolize Arab oil power for the world.
—PETER HOBDAY
British economist

When Ibn Sa'ūd recaptured Riyadh in 1902, he knew that he had to win the confidence of the city's religious scholars, who, as in any Arabian community, were regarded as wise, holy men. These religious elders made up a group called the *ulema.* To win them over, Ibn Sa'ūd promptly married the daughter of the qadi, the chief of the ulema. This qadi was a direct descendant of Muhammad ibn 'Abd al-Wahhāb, the original Wahhabi. The marriage therefore linked the Wahhabi and Saudi families, who together had conquered Arabia a century earlier.

To Ibn Sa'ūd, his new bride was a symbol of coming greatness. Her name was Tarfah, and she bore him a son whom he named Faisal, "the sword," who was probably born in 1905, although some accounts suggest 1904 or 1906 — no precise records of such things were kept in Arabia at the time.

Faisal on a state visit to England in 1932. His early skill as a negotiator led his father, Ibn Sa'ūd, then emir of Riyadh, to appoint him chief ambassador. In 1919, Faisal, then 14 years old, became the first central Arabian in modern times to make a state visit to Europe.

In Allah's help to victory. He helpeth to victory whom He will. He is the Mighty, the Merciful.

—the Koran

Tarfah was not Ibn Sa'ūd's first wife; she was the second of many. Faisal was born into a family that is extraordinarily large and difficult to sort out — even for Arabia, where family relationships can be confusing to outsiders. The confusion stems from two factors. The first is the Arab method of naming. Sons are generally given the names of revered ancestors or heroes, and the same few names are repeated generation after generation, so that a given family may have dozens of members but only a handful of different names. The first name is followed by *ibn*, which means "son of," and the father's name, which in turn may be followed by the grandfather's name and the clan name. Faisal's full name was Faysal ibn 'Abd al-'Azīz ibn 'Abd ar-Rahmān āl-Sa'ūd.

The second factor that makes Ibn Sa'ūd's family difficult for Westerners to sort out is his many marriages. All Muslim males are permitted by their faith to have as many as four wives at any given time, but most are not wealthy enough to support four families. Ibn Sa'ūd's fondness for female companionship was legendary, however, and he acquired his first four wives as soon as he could afford them. Whenever he lost a wife through death or divorce, he remarried quickly. He had 43 sons and at least as many daughters.

At the time of his marriage to Tarfah, Ibn Sa'ūd had three sons by his first wife. Turkī, born in 1900, was his father's heir; his brother Saud was born in 1902. Khalid, the third son, died when he was a baby. Faisal was to have many more brothers, but they were half brothers only — his mother died soon after he was born, without bearing any more children.

Faisal was perhaps too young to grieve for his mother when she died, but her death influenced his life in an important way. The infant was sent to be raised in the household of his mother's family. Although he often visited and traveled with his father and brothers during his childhood, Faisal spent most of his first 12 years in Riyadh, absorbing the teachings of his grandfather Sheik Muhammad ibn 'Abd al-Wahhāb, the most learned and pious man of the community. His education consisted of memorizing the Koran, of learning to eloquently preach, debate, and argue religious subjects with the ulema, and of reading and reciting poetry, which all Arabs love. Faisal also wrote poetry, and early in his life he showed a love of reading and an ability to communicate skillfully. These skills, learned in debate and recitation before his grandfather, later served him well in his diplomatic career.

The Riyadh in which Faisal grew up was nothing like the city of palaces and skyscrapers that is the Saudi capital today. It was a town of one-story, mud-brick houses, with small air holes instead of windows for safety from attack. The town was surrounded by a stone wall. The wall, the houses, and the narrow streets were the same grayish brown color as the surrounding desert. Inside the houses, prayer rugs and floor mats of woven grass were the only furnishings, and painted ceiling-beams the only decorations.

The main gate of the walled city of Riyadh during the the 1940s. Ibn Sa'ūd captured the city in 1902 with a force of just 40 men, only 12 of whom participated in the surprise attack that resulted in the surrender of the garrison. Ibn Sa'ūd made Riyadh his capital; today it is a city of skyscrapers and highways.

A Muslim religious leader holds court in a 1907 painting by the artist L. Deutsch. After Ibn Sa'ūd took Riyadh he won the support of the *ulema*, or council of religious elders, which set legal and social standards for the region. Ibn Sa'ūd married Tarfah, the daughter of the ulema's head; Tarfah later became Faisal's mother.

Life was simple, organized around formal prayers offered five times every day. When not at his studies or performing his religious duties, Faisal shared the pastimes of his brothers and the other boys of Riyadh. These included games of marbles, shooting with a slingshot, climbing palm trees, and trapping and training birds. Every boy dreamed of having his own hunting hawk; Faisal was to have many such birds in his lifetime. At age five or six, boys were mounted on mares for the first time and taught to ride. Turkī, Faisal's oldest brother, had a prize mare said to be the fastest horse in Nejd. To the amazement of his young friends, Faisal one day leapt astride this mettlesome horse and raced it around the town walls without falling.

From his birth, Faisal was said to be small, thin, and of delicate health. Later in life he suffered from a succession of ailments and was never as physically hearty as his father or some of his brothers. Yet those who doubted his courage and strength were often reminded of his headlong gallop around Riyadh on Turkī's mare — and of another incident that happened during Faisal's childhood.

It was the custom of the older boys of Riyadh to tease the younger ones into demonstrating their bravery by jumping into a 30-foot-deep well. The young boys would hold their nose, plunge into the dark waters, and swim around until a rope was lowered with a basket to haul them up. This rite of initiation was frightening and dangerous, and it was not unknown for boys to be hurt or even killed. Yet when Faisal's turn came, he mounted the edge of the well and jumped in coolly and without hesitation. His fearlessness was much admired and long remembered.

During these years, Faisal's father was often away from Riyadh on military expeditions against the Rashids and other clans. Faisal envied Turkī, who was allowed to accompany Ibn Sa'ūd on these expeditions and to live in the military camp. But Faisal saw his father often, whenever Ibn Sa'ūd was in Riyadh. Every evening, Ibn Sa'ūd would send for his small children and play with them for an hour or so after dinner; years later, Faisal followed the same custom. When the children were older, Ibn Sa'ūd took them on excursions outside the city walls. Sometimes he took Faisal up to the cliffs to catch the cool evening air or for a picnic in the gardens and orchards of Wadi al-Hanifa, a nearby valley. As he listened to his father's stories of bedouin and battlefields, and as he watched his father deal diplomatically with the argumentative sheiks and ulema of his growing territory, Faisal absorbed much of Ibn Sa'ūd's pride, sense of honor, and skill in handling men.

Central Arabia in those days had little commerce with the rest of the world. Other nations knew almost nothing of Nejd; only three Europeans had ever seen Riyadh before Faisal's birth, and Faisal's early childhood passed with little awareness of the world outside its walls. But that world was closing in on Arabia, and soon it touched Faisal's life.

Mubarak, the sheik of Kuwait, accepted the protection of the British and permitted them to send a diplomat, called a political agent, to his capital. In 1910, Ibn Sa'ūd and some of his brothers and cousins visited Kuwait and met the British political

Sheikh Mubarak in Kuwait . . . was known to be jealous of Ibn Saud's sudden and spectacular rise to power.

—MOHAMMED ALMANA
Ibn Saud biographer

agent. The agent's name was Captain William Henry Shakespear, and he and Ibn Sa'ūd immediately became friends. Shakespear shared many of the Arab virtues: He was brave, adventurous, solitary by nature, and fond of making long journeys in the desert. So taken was Ibn Sa'ūd with his new friend (probably the first non-Arab the Saudi leader had ever met) that he readily agreed when Shakespear asked for permission to photograph Ibn Sa'ūd and his entourage. This picture, the first ever taken of Ibn Sa'ūd, shows a tall, solemn, handsome man dressed in a gold-trimmed robe and a *kaffiyeh*, the traditional red-and-white checkered Arab headdress.

After the photography ceremony was over, Ibn Sa'ūd invited Shakespear to visit him in Riyadh. Although Shakespear could not do so immediately, the two men remained friends. They met frequently in desert camps over the next few years. One of Shakespear's photographs, taken in front of a goathair tent, shows Ibn Sa'ūd surrounded by his brothers and sons. In the foreground are two young boys; they appear nervous, perhaps fearful of the strange photographic equipment. One of them is Faisal. Shakespear kept voluminous notes of his encounters with the Saudis. His yellowing reports, filed away in the Foreign Office in London, are still the best account of the rise of a new power in central Arabia that occurred around 1910.

This new power was a religious brotherhood, called the Ikhwan (the brethren), descended from the Wahhabi movement of 150 years before. Its emergence fit in well with Ibn Sa'ūd's plans to reorganize Arab society; he hoped to transform the bedouin from a group of nomadic peoples virtually useless to a central government into settled oasis dwellers whose produce and trade could be taxed by such a government. He found the means to do so in the Ikhwan.

Ibn Sa'ūd learned that many especially pious bedouin were joining the Ikhwan. The Ikhwan followed the customs of the Wahhabis — they believed in a strict, pure form of Islam, choosing to wear short, plain robes as a symbol of their disdain for worldly goods and declaring jihad on fellow Arabs who did not share the beliefs of their sect. Like his distant ancestor Muhammad ibn Sa'ūd, Ibn Sa'ūd realized that militant religious belief was a powerful weapon. He decided to ally himself with the Ikhwan and turn them into an army.

In 1912, he granted the oasis of Artawiya to Ikhwan settlers. More such settlements followed; within a few years, there were as many as 100 Ikhwan communities scattered across Nejd, peopled by men who combined the toughness and fighting skills of the bedouin with fierce loyalty to Ibn Sa'ūd. In 1913, the Ikhwan helped Ibn Sa'ūd drive the Turks out of the al-Hasa region on the Persian Gulf — a region that would become enormously important decades later, when oil was discovered there.

A typical bedouin family in the Arabian desert in the 1920s. Central Arabian nomads lived as camel herders, caravan traders, and bandits; frequent warfare, brigandage, and the inhospitality of the landscape kept the region isolated from foreign visitors for hundreds of years.

Captain Shakespear photographed the Ikhwan army on the march, with robed warriors mounted on their swiftest camels and war banners streaming in the wind.

It was several years before Shakespear could get permission from his superiors in India to accept Ibn Sa'ūd's invitation to visit Riyadh. The British government wanted to avoid stirring up the tribes of Arabia because such activities might bring trouble between Britain and Turkey. Shakespear was ordered not to be too friendly with the Saudis; the other tribes in the peninsula might complain to the Turks. But with the outbreak of World War I in 1914, the brittle relationship between Britain and Turkey was shattered as the two nations found themselves on opposite sides. Suddenly, Captain Shakespear's friendship with Ibn Sa'ūd was valuable to the British, who sent him to Riyadh to recruit the Saudis' assistance against the Turks.

Elements of the Arab army in the Hejaz region of Arabia during World War I. The Arabs, including those led by Ibn Sa'ūd, fought alongside the British in the Middle Eastern theater of the war. Arab fighters were instrumental in ousting the Turks from the Middle East.

It was now eight years since the Saudis had killed ibn Rashid in battle. Supported by Turkish soldiers and money, however, the Rashids were threatening to recapture Nejd from the Saudis; Ibn Sa'ūd replied by mustering a force of about 6,000 to attack the combined Turkish-Rashid force. When Shakespear at last reached Riyadh, the city and the camp outside it bustled with military activity. Although Ibn Sa'ūd urged him to return to the safety of Kuwait, Shakespear was determined to stay with the Saudis and fight with them. His reasons remain unclear to this day. Perhaps he was acting as an agent of Britain, hoping to secure Ibn Sa'ūd's friendship for his country. Perhaps he acted out of admiration for the Saudi leader or out of the sheer love of adventure. Whatever his motive, he marched with Ibn Sa'ūd's army.

In January 1915, a battle took place at Jarrab, north of Riyadh. Shakespear was directing the Saudi gunners when suddenly some of Ibn Sa'ūd's allies broke rank and fled without warning. The Rashids swept across the field, killing the British officer in the process. Ibn Sa'ūd wept when he learned of Shakespear's death, and years later he still wept when he thought of him. The political agent won little fame in his own country, however. In 1928, a British diplomat who asked Ibn Sa'ūd to name the Englishman he most admired was mistakenly impressed with the Arab's literary passion when Ibn Sa'ūd answered, "Shakespear," and burst into tears. Captain Shakespear, a distant descendant of the famous playwright, had already been forgotten.

Jarrab was only a temporary setback for the Saudis. As World War I raged on, Arabs throughout Arabia and the Middle East joined with the British to defeat the Turks. The world remembers the Arab Revolt largely because of the British officer T. E. Lawrence — Lawrence of Arabia. His activities, however, took place in the Hejaz, far from Nejd, fighting alongside a clan called the Hashemites, who would eventually become the rulers of Jordan.

Meanwhile, Nejd was not much involved in the world war. Ibn Sa'ūd was busy trouncing rebellious

[Captain Shakespear] had insisted upon accompanying Ibn Saud on the expedition against Ibn Rashid, and had been determined to take part in the battle even though the Prince urged him to stay out of danger.

—MOHAMMED ALMANA
Ibn Saud biographer

British captain T. E. Lawrence, better known as Lawrence of Arabia, led Arab troops against the Turks in heavy fighting in Hejaz. In Nejd, the region controlled by Ibn Sa'ūd (the British recognized his rule in a 1915 treaty), there was little fighting against the Turks; instead Ibn Sa'ūd used his troops to solidify his rule over rebellious tribes.

local tribes — including the one that had deserted the field at Jarrab — and the Turks made no attempt to recapture Nejd. At the end of the war in 1918, Ibn Sa'ūd controlled Nejd and al-Hasa more firmly than ever. He was, however, eager for a formal treaty with Britain that would result in an annual subsidy, or cash payment, of foreign aid. He also wanted the British to know that the Hashemites were not the only power in Arabia. He therefore was delighted to learn from Harry St. John Philby, Britain's new agent in Riyadh, that the British government was arranging visits to London for its wartime allies, including Nejd.

Ibn Sa'ūd announced that the Nejdi ambassador to London would be his son and heir, Turkī, a proven warrior who was much loved by the Saudis and the Ikhwan. The visit was scheduled for 1919, but Turkī never made the journey; he died in late 1918, one of the millions who succumbed to the worldwide epidemic of Spanish influenza. His grieving father declared that Faisal, then 14, would make the trip in his place. In selecting Faisal as his ambassador, Ibn Sa'ūd bypassed his second son, Saud, who was somewhat shy and inarticulate. His choice of the alert, well-spoken Faisal was a good one, yet it planted the seed of future discord between the brothers.

Faisal was not to travel alone, of course. He was accompanied by his companion and bodyguard Murzouq, a black slave who had grown up with Faisal; by an al-Hasa merchant who was to make purchases for Ibn Sa'ūd; by an older cousin, Ahmad al-Thunayan, who had been coached in Ibn Sa'ūd's policies; and by a handful of other slaves who acted as the delegation's bodyguards. The group, called the Central Arabian Mission, was shepherded by Philby and another British diplomat, who provided interpreters, as none of the Arabs spoke English.

[The Ikhwan] movement became a weapon in the hands of Ibn Saud.
—MOHAMMED ALMANA
Ibn Saud biographer

The trip must have been quite an adventure for a teenage boy who had never been in a boat, never seen an automobile or a telephone, and never seen more than one or two foreigners. The Central Arabian Mission went first by steamboat to Bombay, India, where they were to board a larger ship for England. Although Faisal was ill during the journey to Bombay, he worked diligently at what the British diplomats called "the knife and fork drill." The British envoys knew that their Arabian charges would suffer a great loss of dignity in Europe if they continued to eat in the Arab fashion, with the fingers of their right hand. When they arrived in Bombay and sat down for their first hotel dinner, Faisal and Ahmad were shocked to see the diplomats and the other British guests help themselves to asparagus with their fingers, as is the British custom with that slippery vegetable. The Arabs, determined to behave correctly, continued to saw and poke with the unfamiliar new implements.

Faisal presented King George V of Britain with a sword and a gold, jewel-encrusted scabbard during his diplomatic trip to London in 1919. In return, the British monarch gave the 14-year-old Arabian ambassador signed photographs of himself and the queen.

This incident was the first of many surprises that Faisal encountered in the world outside Arabia. He rode a train and an elephant in India, trudged uncomplainingly through rain and fog in London, and put up with the bungling efforts of the British Foreign Office to find lodging for the mission. Unfortunately, many hotels refused to accommodate the Arabs, even as guests of the government. These refusals may have had something to do with the loud, wailing calls to prayer that echoed up and down the halls five times every day or with Murzouq and the rest of the slaves' insistence upon sleeping in the halls outside their masters' doorways and kindling open fires to brew coffee. Finally, Philby found lodging for the delegation in an army officers' hotel.

Not long after his arrival in London, Faisal was invited to meet King George V in Buckingham Palace. He presented the king with a gift from Ibn Sa'ūd: a sword whose sheath was of solid gold encrusted with pearls. In return he received signed photographs of the king and queen. Soon after, Faisal and Ahmad were received by Lord Curzon, Britain's foreign minister. Although Faisal was young, he was acting as his father's official ambassador and was well aware of the dignity of this role. When Lord Curzon patronizingly offered him a piece of candy, Faisal stormed out of his office. Ahmad later demanded an apology from the British government.

The candy was not at the root of the Arabs' disappointment with Britain. They were upset because Sharif Husain ibn Ali, the leader of the Hashemite clan, had begun calling himself king of the Arabs and Britain had done nothing about it. The British, in fact, were urging Ibn Sa'ūd to remain on friendly terms with the Hashemites. But throughout the remainder of the trip, Ahmad spoke often of Saudi ambitions and the coming growth of the Saudi state, which, he said, would soon be more powerful than the Hashemites. The British failed to take him seriously and were to regret it later.

In addition to these official visits, Faisal's itinerary included many events that were planned to entertain and impress him. He and his party visited the zoo, where Faisal fled in alarm from a charging sea lion, and the Royal Observatory at Greenwich, where they were amazed to see stars in the daytime through a telescope. They were taken aboard a captured German submarine, filmed there, and shown the film later in a theater. They attended a performance of *The Mikado*, a comic operetta, and applauded politely at jokes they did not understand. They visited an automobile factory, which greatly impressed the merchant from al-Hasa; several years later he succeeded in bringing the first automobile to Nejd, although it had to be dragged across the sand dunes by camels. They saw the Parliament buildings, a steel plant in Wales, and Mount Snowdon, England's highest mountain. Faisal was invited to climb Snowdon, and he gamely hitched up his robes and started up the hill. It was now November, however, and the climbing party soon encountered a snowstorm — something that must have been especially unpleasant for a lifelong desert dweller. Faisal gave up the climb and was hurried back to his hotel.

On several occasions, Faisal managed to surprise his hosts in return. At the zoo, he shocked bystanders when he remarked that a stuffed gorilla reminded him of one of the slaves at home. When he was offered tea at Parliament, he poured the contents of the sugar bowl into his cup — probably a month's supply of sugar, which was rationed at that time because of war shortages. And, upon being asked which of the many sights he had seen in England had impressed him most, he calmly replied, "The moving staircase at Piccadilly Circus." He had sneaked away from his escorts one afternoon and spent hours riding up and down the escalators.

Hoarded money never does anyone any good.
—IBN SAUD

Philby was a good host. He tried to make the Arabs as comfortable as possible, and he was genuinely devoted to the interests of Ibn Sa'ūd. A few years later, in fact, he became a Muslim, abandoned his position in the British government, and lived out the rest of his life in Arabia as an adviser to the court of Ibn Sa'ūd. In 1919, however, he contented himself with showing Faisal and Ahmad around his old college at Cambridge. He also took the Arabs to Eastbourne, where his son, Kim Philby, attended school. A photograph taken on the occasion shows the Philbys and the Arabs posing for a group portrait, with two boys of about the same age in the front row, Faisal in glittering royal robes with his hand on his sword hilt, Kim in a schoolboy's jacket and round Eton collar. (Kim Philby grew up to become one of Britain's top intelligence agents while at the same time serving as a mole for Soviet intellignce; in the 1950s he defected to Moscow, where he died 30 years later.)

A young Faisal in London after World War I. Assigned by his father to be the Nejdi ambassador, Faisal was taken to India and then to London by British diplomats in 1919. Faisal's trip was intended to convince the British to support the Saudi family over the Hashemites, who ruled Hejaz.

After several hectic weeks in England, the Central Arabian Mission went to Europe so that Ahmad and Faisal could be present at the Versailles peace conference in Paris, where the victorious nations of World War I were meeting to divide the spoils of the postwar world. Ahmad and Faisal played no real part in the peace settlements, however, and their one interview with the Hashemites ended in indignation when one of the Hashemites made fun of Ahmad's long beard.

While in Europe, Faisal toured some of the great battlefields of the world war: Amiens, Verdun, Strasbourg. They wandered amid the rubble of bombed villages and the thousands of wooden crosses marking the mass graves of fallen soldiers. Faisal was shaken by this evidence of warfare on a scale larger and more impersonal than the Arabs had dreamed of. From that point on, he was modest about his own battle experiences and said that they were "nothing much."

Finally, it was time to return to Riyadh. The Central Arabian Mission took ship in December from Marseilles, France. Despite the culture shock he must have experienced, Faisal had carried out his first official mission with self-possession and style. The trip marked the beginning of his 57-year career as his people's representative abroad, and it also made him one of the first Saudis to have firsthand knowledge of the wide world beyond Arabia.

The Versailles peace conference of 1919, in which the victorious nations of World War I redistributed many of the holdings of the vanquished nations. Faisal briefly attended the conference outside Paris; it was his first taste of international diplomacy on a grand scale.

4

The Last Conquests

[While Ibn Saud] sought the support of the British his dealings with them were complicated by the rivalry with Hussein of Mecca.
—PETER HOBDAY
British economist

On February 12, 1920, Faisal and his entourage returned to Arabia at Hofuf, a city near the Persian Gulf coast. He was greeted by his father, who was delighted to see that the young man appeared to be in good health after his travels. But while Ibn Sa'ūd was pleased with Faisal's health and with the reports he had received of his son's dignified behavior, he was less pleased to learn that the British would strongly disapprove of any Saudi ventures against the Hashemites.

In fact, the Hashemites were high in British favor. In May 1921, a council of British diplomats under Winston Churchill met in Cairo and carved up the Arab territories of the former Ottoman Empire into new nations — the nations that continue to shape the politics of the Middle East today. Syria and Lebanon were turned over to French administration;

Ibn Sa'ūd (left foreground) stands next to the sheik of Bahrain in 1928, two years after Ibn Sa'ūd had conquered Mecca and added the Hejaz region to his dominions. In the 1920s, Faisal's father extended his rule over most of present-day Saudi Arabia.

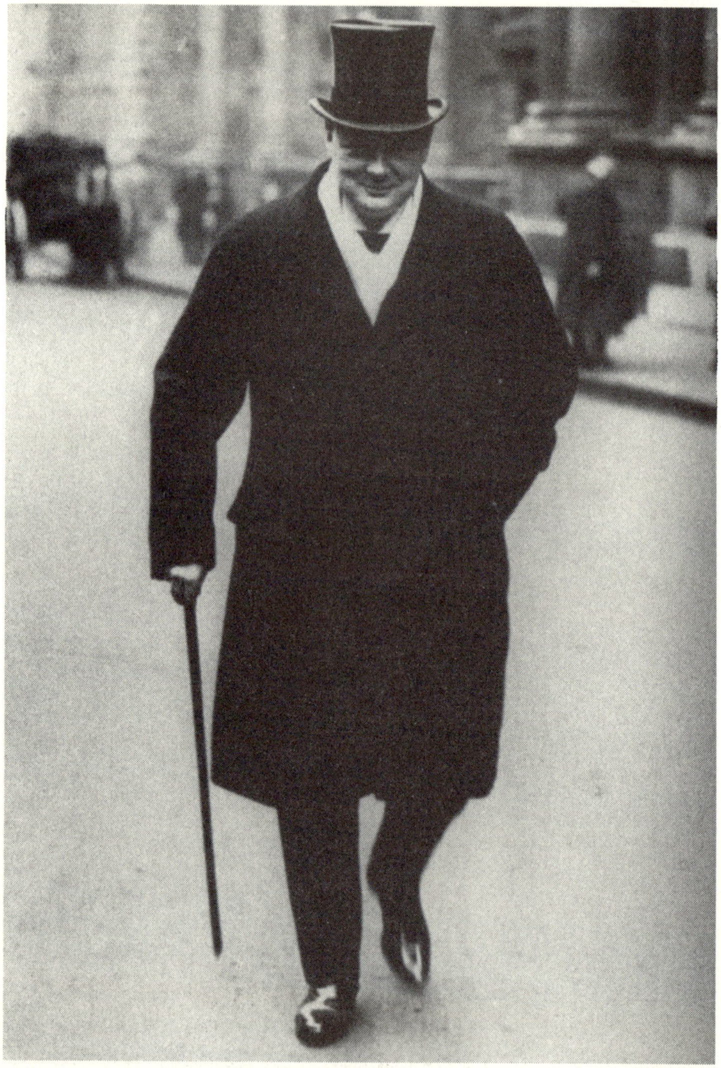

Winston Churchill, head of the British Colonial Office, in 1921, when he presided over an agreement that divided the former Turkish colonies in the Middle East. France received Syria and Lebanon, Britain received Palestine, and members of the Hashemite clan — bitter rivals of the Saudi clan — were made rulers of Iraq, Transjordan, and Hejaz.

Palestine, which would later become the state of Israel, was put under British mandate; the region called Mesopotamia was renamed Iraq, and a Hashemite was made its king; the area between Syria, Palestine, and Iraq was named Transjordan (present-day Jordan) and given to another Hashemite to rule; and the Hashemite leader himself, Sharif Husain ibn Ali, was confirmed as king of Hejaz.

The British, meanwhile, acknowledged Ibn Sa'ūd as the emir of Riyadh and left his rule of Nejd unchallenged. When he heard of the council and its results, Ibn Sa'ūd sneered at the idea of the British parceling out kingships to their favorites. Nevertheless, seeing that the Hashemites had full British support, he decided to turn his attention elsewhere.

As a first step, he concentrated on the province of Asir, a small area along the Red Sea coast of Arabia, sandwiched between Hejaz on the north and Yemen on the south. The area had been ruled by a clan called the Aidh until the early 19th century, when a religious leader called the Idrisi arrived in Asir from North Africa, took over, and established an Idrisi line of rulers that held control ever since. In 1920, the remaining Aidh chieftains sought Ibn Sa'ūd's help in expelling the Idrisi. Ibn Sa'ūd sent Ikhwan warriors to help the Aidh, including a large force under Faisal. As Faisal was only 15 years old and had no experience in military command, Ibn Sa'ūd provided him with a seasoned adviser.

The village of Abu-Arish in the Arabian region of Asir. In 1920, Ibn Sa'ūd used a local power struggle as a pretext for attacking Asir, a remote mountain area in the southwestern corner of what is today Saudi Arabia. Faisal participated in the successful campaign to annex Asir.

Faisal's march on the coast was carried out in good order — although some of the Saudis suffered from malaria in the damp lowland plain, which was very different from their native climate — and succeeded in routing the Idrisi's forces. But then Ibn Sa'ūd sprang a surprise upon the Aidh: He annexed Asir, adding it to his own territory. The Aidh chieftains, two brothers named Hassan and Muhammad, were taken to Riyadh. Ibn Sa'ūd told them that Saudi rule was necessary to keep the Idrisi from returning and also to keep the king of Hejaz from encroaching upon Asir. Hassan and Muhammad were allowed to return to Asir, but as private citizens only. They had no choice but to accept the rule of a governor appointed by Ibn Sa'ūd. Faisal's first military venture was thus considered a rousing success.

Next, Ibn Sa'ūd looked to the north. He marshaled the Ikhwan in the summer of 1921 and advanced to the town of Hail. There the descendants of ibn Rashid, Ibn Sa'ūd's old enemy, clung tenaciously to a large, arid territory that ran north to the borders of Iraq and Transjordan. For two decades, Ibn Sa'ūd had been too busy in central Arabia to worry about this desolate northern district, which the ancient Romans had called Arabia Petraea, or "stony Arabia." Now, however, he was determined to conquer this last Rashid stronghold.

In linking himself so strongly with the Hashemites, Al Aidh gravely misjudged the mood of his people.

—MOHAMMED ALMANA
Ibn Saud biographer

The Rashids themselves had made it easy for him. They had always been a quarrelsome clan, often divided by internal fighting; in the 90 years before 1920, they had had 14 rulers, only 2 of whom had died of natural causes. In the spring of 1920, during a family shooting-contest, the emir of Hail had been foolish enough to insult a cousin's marksmanship. The offended cousin promptly demonstrated the accuracy of his aim by drilling the emir through the forehead with a single shot.

When Ibn Sa'ūd's army arrived at the gates of Hail a year later, the local inhabitants, fearing the wrath of the Ikhwan and tired of the unstable Rashids, submitted immediately. Ibn Sa'ūd incorporated the region into Nejd, thus doubling his territory, and changed his title from emir of Riyadh to sultan of Nejd.

Faisal's second military mission came about in 1924 and took him again to Asir, where Hassan and Muhammad, the Aidh chieftains, were leading a rebellion among their former subjects. Hearing of unrest in Asir, the exiled Idrisi and some of his followers crossed the Red Sea from Egypt in the hope of regaining their former power. Ibn Sa'ūd sent Faisal, now 19, to the province with enough troops to quell the revolt quickly and easily. The rebellion was soon crushed, but instead of executing Hassan and Muhammad, Faisal sent them to Riyadh, where they were compelled to remain under Ibn Sa'ūd's watchful eye.

By this time, Faisal had become his father's trusted lieutenant. He shared Ibn Sa'ūd's burning ambition: to restore the full greatness of the old Saudi empire — which meant gaining control of Hejaz. Once Hail and Asir were firmly under Saudi rule,

Two of Ibn Sa'ūd's bodyguards. Around 1910, Ibn Sa'ūd obtained the support of the Ikhwan, a religious brotherhood of bedouin warriors who adhered to Wahhabism, the strict, conservative form of Islam practiced by the majority of central Arabians. The Ikhwan formed the backbone of Ibn Sa'ūd's fighting force.

An encampment of Ibn Sa'ūd's troops in northern Arabia, during the 1921 campaign that resulted in the taking of Hail and the doubling of Ibn Sa'ūd's territory. Three years later Faisal put down a revolt in Asir and earned the status of his father's most trusted confidant.

Ibn Sa'ūd was again skirmishing with Sharif Husain ibn Ali, the Hashemite leader, over control of several oases on the border between Hejaz and Nejd. At about the same time, Britain announced that it was ending financial aid to both the sharif and Ibn Sa'ūd. Although it still maintained a protective interest over Kuwait, Iraq, Palestine, and Jordan, Britain now seemed content to let affairs inside the Arabian Peninsula settle themselves without outside interference. Sensing that Britain's support of the sharif had slackened, Ibn Sa'ūd waited for his opportunity—and soon the sharif handed it to him.

In March 1924, Muslims all over the world learned that Mustafa Kemal (later known as Atatürk), the leader of Turkey after the fall of the Ottoman Empire, had given up the position of caliph, or spiritual head of the Islamic faith, which had been held by Turkish leaders for more than four centuries. Sharif ibn Ali immediately claimed that he was now the caliph, saying that it was his right as king of the holy cities of Mecca and Medina. Many Muslims, including many Hejazi, viewed the sharif's act as one of unspeakable vanity. Most displeased of all were Ibn Sa'ūd and the Ikhwan, who regarded the Hashemites as impure Muslims, given to such sinful luxuries as smoking tobacco and even, perhaps, drinking alcohol. The Ikhwan believed that under Hashemite rule the holy cities were mismanaged and worldly, and they longed to take over and run things their way.

Ibn Sa'ūd knew this, and he also knew that Sharif ibn Ali's claim to the caliphate was just the excuse he needed to launch a jihad against the sharif. Soon after the sharif proclaimed himself caliph, Ibn Sa'ūd's Ikhwan armies were on the march.

But the Saudi campaign against Hejaz did not go altogether smoothly. Ibn Sa'ūd wanted to give the post of chief military commander to Faisal and to have Saud, Faisal's older brother, remain in Nejd as his father's deputy. Saud protested his father's decision, and in the end neither of the sons marched with the army. But the conflict suggested a growing rivalry between the brothers that, years later, would threaten to tear the family—and the nation—apart.

New Turkish president Mustafa Kemal (later known as Atatürk), and his wife Latife, in 1923, the year he began his drive to westernize Turkey. One of his first moves was to give up the post of caliph, or worldwide spiritual head of the Islamic faith, which had been held by Turkish leaders for more than 400 years.

Part of the interior of the Grand Mosque at Mecca in the late 1920s. After Mustafa Kemal gave up the caliphate, Sharif Husain ibn Ali, the Hashemite ruler of Hejaz, proclaimed himself the new caliph — a move seen by the Ikhwan as blasphemous. Ibn Sa'ūd used them to invade Hejaz in 1924; after taking Mecca and Jidda, the region was his.

The Ikhwan's initial advance was upon Taif, a garrison town on the way to Mecca. It should have been defended by one of Sharif ibn Ali's sons, but he and his army fled the town as the Ikhwan approached. Upon finding Taif undefended, the Ikhwan entered the town and slaughtered some 300 civilians.

Ibn Sa'ūd was appalled to hear of the massacre; perhaps too late, he wished that he had given the command to Faisal after all. At any rate, he ordered Faisal to hasten to Mecca to prevent any Ikhwan outrages there. The fanatical fighting force he had created was becoming ungovernable.

Order was restored when Faisal reached Mecca. The sharif fled to Jidda; soon after, he boarded a British steamer — with, it is said, a procession of slaves carrying 800,000 gold coins in tightly welded kerosene cans — to live out his life in luxury on the island of Cyprus. In his absence, Faisal and Ibn Sa'ūd were able to enter Mecca quietly, in humble pilgrim's robes, without a shot being fired.

Mecca surrendered peacefully to the Saudis, but Ibn Sa'ūd could not claim to control Hejaz until he had also taken the nearby port city of Jidda, as well as Medina and its port city, Yenbo'. Muhammad, five years younger than Faisal and next in succession, commanded a force that easily took Medina and Yenbo' after promising that the wild Ikhwan would not be allowed to enter the cities. Jidda, however, was a more difficult proposition altogether.

Jidda was Arabia's most cosmopolitan city — more open to the traders and diplomats of the world than any other. Merchants and consuls of many countries lived in Jidda, and Ibn Sa'ūd knew that a rash attack on the city could cause difficulties with foreign governments if some of the foreign residents were killed. So he sent Faisal to Jidda with strict orders to besiege the city but not to assault it.

Faisal carried out his father's orders well. He surrounded Jidda. First, water grew scarce in the city, then food and other supplies. Famine and disease spread. By the end of 1925, the city capitulated when Ali, Sharif ibn Ali's son, turned Jidda over to Faisal and fled to Iraq, where one of his brothers was king. The entire Hejaz region was now controlled by Ibn Sa'ūd.

On January 8, 1926, a great ceremony took place in the courtyard of the Grand Mosque in Mecca. Accompanied by the mosque's *imam*, or prayer leader, Ibn Sa'ūd stepped forward. The imam proclaimed him king of Hejaz, and all the citizens of the city and the outlying region moved forward one by one to shake their new king's hand and swear *bay ah*, the Arabian oath of loyalty. Twenty-four years after his daring capture of Riyadh, Ibn Sa'ūd, king of Hejaz and sultan of Nejd, had succeeded in rebuilding the ancient Saudi empire.

Faisal was at his father's side to observe how he set about governing his new territory. Now that his lifelong ambition had been achieved, Ibn Sa'ūd showed himself to be a moderate and prudent ruler. He was aware that the rest of the world took a greater interest in Hejaz than in Nejd, partly because of the trade and diplomatic interests in Jidda and partly because all Muslim nations cared deeply about their holy cities. For the first time, Ibn Sa'ūd entered into formal diplomatic relations with other nations. As soon as he was proclaimed king of Hejaz, the Soviet Union officially recognized his government and appointed an ambassador. Other countries soon followed suit.

Saud, Faisal's older brother and heir to Ibn Sa'ūd's sultanate, stands with a group of his advisers in the late 1920s. Saud, who is believed to have resented his father's greater trust in Faisal, proved his skill in desert warfare when he helped put down an Ikhwan revolt in 1932.

Faisal preparing to embark on a 1926 diplomatic trip to Britain as his father's official foreign minister, a post to which he was appointed in 1924. That same year he was named viceroy of Hejaz, giving him administrative control of Mecca and Medina and of the taxes paid by Muslim pilgrims to the two holy cities.

Ibn Sa'ūd realized that he needed an official representative in Jidda to deal with these ambassadors and their governments. Faisal was the obvious choice. He had demonstrated the necessary qualities of self-assurance and diplomacy. He thoroughly understood his father's wishes and followed them to the letter. And he had already had some experience with foreigners and their customs. Accordingly, his father named him viceroy of Hejaz and foreign minister for Hejaz and Nejd.

In the autumn of 1926, Faisal made a second trip to Europe, this time in his official role as foreign minister. After a month or so in England and the Netherlands, he returned to begin the duties that were to occupy him in Mecca and Jidda for nearly three decades.

In 1927, Ibn Sa'ūd dropped the title of sultan and named himself king of Nejd and Hejaz. Faisal, the viceroy of Hejaz, also served as foreign minister of both regions. It was clear that Ibn Sa'ūd wanted to unify the regions into a single kingdom, but the process of unification had to wait until Ibn Sa'ūd had dealt with a new enemy — his erstwhile allies, the Ikhwan.

For some time, the Ikhwan had been chafing under Ibn Sa'ūd's rule. They were religious extremists, and they now felt that their king, while pious enough by the standards of Muslims from such "lax" countries as Lebanon and Egypt, was too moderate to suit them. He tried to humor them in small ways, such as the public destruction of the record player he liked to listen to in his tent, but he could not permit their harassment of pilgrims from more liberal or modernized countries. This angered the Ikhwan, who had expected to be able to force their own customs on everyone in Mecca.

For decades, Ibn Sa'ūd had groomed the Ikhwan as a fighting force, but now that Nejd, Asir, Hail, and Hejaz had all been conquered and the fighting was over, the Ikhwan resorted to raids across the border into Iraq, stealing sheep and sometimes slaughtering innocent peasants. Ibn Sa'ūd punished the leaders of the raids, which made the Ikhwan increasingly dissatisfied with the Saudis. In 1929, several Ikhwan leaders rallied their followers to revolt against Ibn Sa'ūd.

> ***[Ibn Saud] entered the Holy City, not as a conquering monarch, but with bared head and dressed in the simple robes of a pilgrim.***
>
> —MOHAMMED ALMANA
> Ibn Saud biographer

The revolt flared and sputtered for several years in the desert and the oases, and Ibn Sa'ūd was forced to send several punitive expeditions against the army he had created. His Saudi army was larger and better armed than the rebel force; his troops now had armored cars and machine guns, while the Ikhwan had only camels and rifles. Many Ikhwan were killed and their settlements destroyed. Some of these expeditions were led by Ibn Sa'ūd's oldest son, Saud, who proved himself competent enough at conducting small-scale desert maneuvers—Saud, in fact, was always more comfortable in the desert and among the bedouin than in cities and among foreigners. Finally, by 1932, the Ikhwan rebellion was fully subdued.

That same year, Ibn Sa'ūd realized his life's ambition: the unification of Arabia. On September 18, he announced to the world that his various territories had been combined into a single country called the Kingdom of Saudi Arabia. It was, and remains today, the only nation in the world named after a family. At the same time, he formally designated Saud as the heir to the throne.

5

The Kingdom

He whom Allah guideth, he indeed is led aright, and he whom He sendeth astray, for him thou wilt not find a guiding friend.
—the Koran

The new nation of Saudi Arabia soon received diplomatic recognition from the other countries of the world; again, the Soviet Union was first. Faisal embarked on a diplomatic tour of European capitals. This time, he visited Moscow in acknowledgement of the Soviets' recognition of the new Saudi nation and toured the Soviet Union's southern republics, where many of the people are Muslim. Nevertheless, relations between Saudi Arabia and the Soviet Union would never become warm. Unlike the Muslims of Egypt and Syria, who would later be strongly influenced by Soviet communism, the Saudis would always remain firmly opposed to any system of government that endorses atheism, the denial of the existence of God. As king, Faisal would view the Soviet Union as an enemy and a dangerous presence in the Middle East.

Ibn Sa'ūd (left) proclaimed himself monarch of the new kingdom of Saudi Arabia on September 10, 1932, and installed his son Saud (right) as crown prince and heir to the throne. Saudi Arabia, named after its ruling family, remained a fundamentally family-run entity through the 1980s.

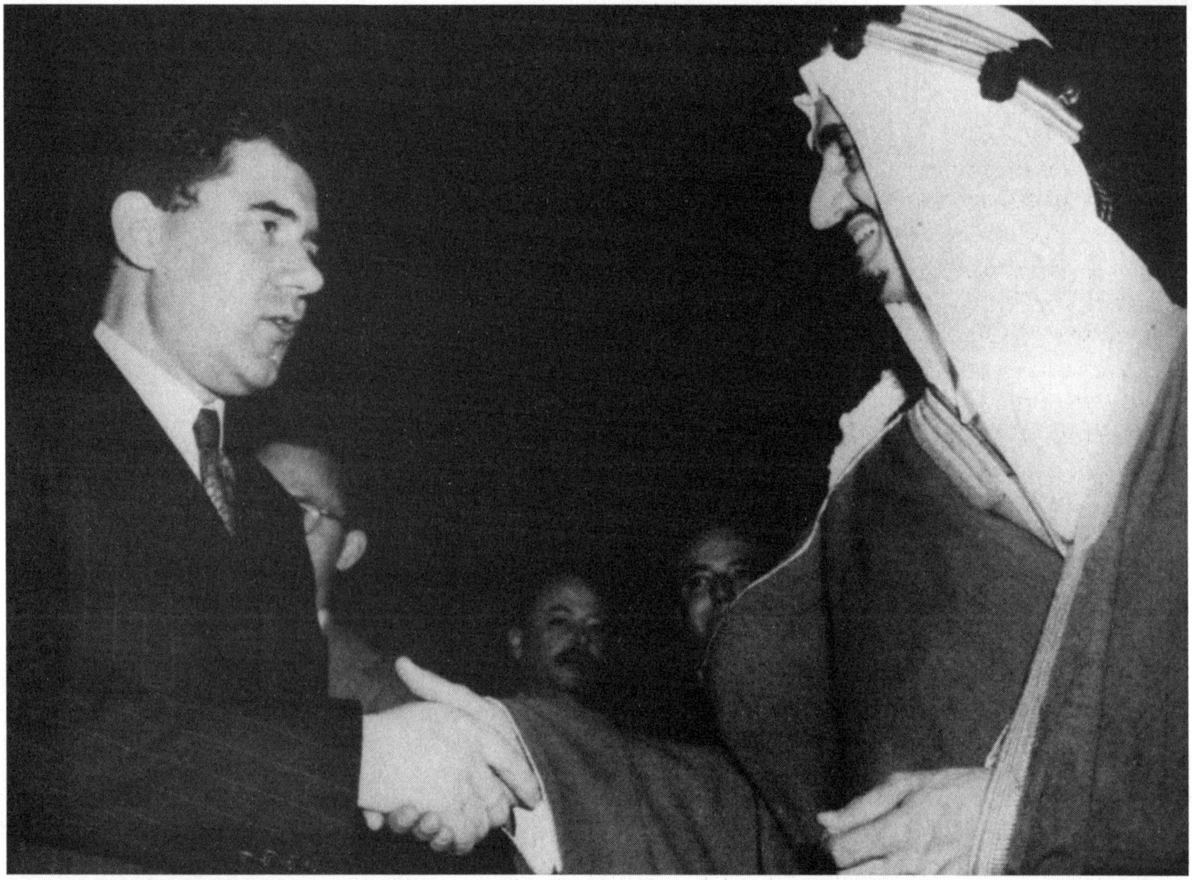

Faisal meets Soviet diplomat Andrei A. Gromyko in New York in 1947. In 1932 the Soviet Union became the first country to recognize Saudi Arabia, but the Saudis never developed close relations with the Soviets' socialist government.

Faisal's 1932 European trip was made for diplomatic purposes, but it also brought him a new wife. He had already been married twice, but both marriages were made for political purposes, as was often the case among Saudi princes and princesses; marriage was regarded as a good way to seal an alliance or to heal a rift between enemy clans. Faisal's first wife had borne his oldest son, Abdullah. His second wife had been a member of the powerful Jaluwi clan, allies of the Saudis from the time of the capture of Riyadh. This marriage had produced two more sons, Khalid and Saud. Some of Faisal's eight daughters were born during these marriages as well, but information about Saudi princesses is considered private and is rarely available outside the family.

Faisal's third wife was a young woman he met in Istanbul, Turkey, on his way home from his diplomatic tour. Her name was Iffat al-Thunayan, and she was the niece of Ahmad al-Thunayan, who had accompanied him on his trip to London in 1919. She and her mother had lived in Turkey for years.

Her father had recently died, but the inheritance of some land he owned near Taif was in dispute. Iffat's mother, hearing that the Saudi king's third son was passing through Istanbul, called on him to ask for his help in straightening out her property claim. Faisal was much taken with his visitor's daughter and invited both women to come to Jidda, where it would be easier to resolve the dispute. Soon after their arrival in Jidda, Faisal married Iffat.

Faisal is generally believed to have settled down with Iffat, living quite happily with her alone. Her influence on the life of Saudi Arabian women was to be a great one, and she alone, of all the Saudi royal wives, was called queen by the people, even though that formal title does not exist in Saudi Arabia.

Faisal and his new wife maintained a number of residences. They made their home in Mecca in the viceroy's palace, and from there Faisal administered the affairs of the province. When he had time, the prince pursued his reading of Arab poetry and religion, and he often said how pleasant it was to read the Koran in the Prophet's own city. He had little time for such scholarly pleasures, however, because he also spent much time in Jidda, acting as foreign minister. There he set up his offices in a palace that the people soon referred to as the Viceroy's Lodge. His home in Jidda was a modest villa outside the city.

I hereby appoint my sons Saud and Faisal to lead our forces.
—IBN SAUD
before the invasion of Yemen

He also maintained a small palace in Riyadh, which had been made capital of the new nation. This palace was built, like all the buildings at that time, of mud-brick, with thick walls for coolness, many small courtyards so that the members of the family could find privacy, and a *majlis*, or council room, where the head of the household served coffee to visitors and advisers every evening.

The 1930s were a time of happiness for Faisal as he enjoyed his marriage with Iffat and administering his portion of his father's kingdom in the dual role of viceroy and foreign minister. He settled disputes between merchants and the ulema. He held his own with foreign diplomats. Above all, he sharpened his negotiating skills as a fund-raiser, seeking loans from other nations.

At this time, Saudi Arabia's only sources of income were the head tax, a small yearly payment required of every citizen, and the taxes and fees paid by Muslims making the pilgrimage to Mecca and Medina. Ibn Sa'ūd had enjoyed his cash subsidies from the British. He spent the money lavishly and without much thought for the future, hosting huge banquets daily to feed as many as 300 guests and rewarding wandering poets with handfuls of gold coins. Now that the British aid had ended, he needed money simply to maintain his kingdom. Faisal, his foreign minister, was too smart, however, to accept foreign loans that would tie Saudi Arabia too closely to other nations. Ibn Sa'ūd, therefore, was forced to look elsewhere for a source of cash, and he found one right under his feet.

British diplomat Harry St. John Philby, who a few years earlier converted to Islam and moved to Saudi Arabia, in 1938. In the early 1930s, Philby set up a bidding war between U.S. and British oil companies for rights to potential Saudi petroleum deposits.

Oil had been found in great quantities in Iraq years before. For some time, geologists had speculated that oil might also lie nearer the Persian Gulf in Arabia. Some places in Nejd, especially in the al-Hasa region near the coast, were known to have springs of pitch, a form of petroleum tar that wells up from beneath the ground. These seepages of pitch usually meant that petroleum deposits were nearby. In the early 1930s, Ibn Sa'ūd permitted several geologists to survey parts of his kingdom. He knew that they were looking for oil, but he did not expect them to find it — nor did he fully understand how valuable it might prove to be. "Just find me some wells of water for my people," he begged the geologists, and he was delighted when they did so.

By 1932, the presence of these geologists in Arabia had given rise to rumors that oil had been found there. Several foreign companies became interested in getting the Saudi oil concession, a form of contract in which a foreign company provides the money and skill necessary to extract the oil and shares the profits with the country that owns it. At this time Harry St. John Philby, the British diplomat who had become a Muslim and now lived in Saudi Arabia, entered the picture.

Philby orchestrated a bidding war that pitted the British against the Americans. Companies from both countries sent representatives to Jidda, but only Philby was allowed to approach the king directly. He knew that Ibn Sa'ūd did not really care who got the concession, so long as he got the best price for it. The king, in fact, doubted whether the oil really existed. After months of negotiation, during which Philby bustled importantly from Jidda to Riyadh and back, each side made its final offer. The Americans, a team of companies headed by Standard Oil, offered a down payment five times greater than that offered by the British. The U.S. companies were willing to pay about $250,000 — and they agreed to pay in gold coins, the only kind of money that Ibn Sa'ūd really trusted.

Philby passed the American contract on to Abdullah Suleiman, the king's finance minister, who read it aloud to Ibn Sa'ūd. As he droned on through clause after clause of fine print, the king dozed off. When Suleiman fell silent, the king awoke with a start. He turned to his roomful of advisers and asked whether they approved of the contract. As he expected, they all nodded yes. "Very well," he told Suleiman. "Put your trust in Allah and sign." And that was the beginning of Saudi Arabia's petropower and petrodollars.

Everybody in the court was glad that the Americans seemed likely to get the concession, for we all felt that the British were still tainted by colonialism. If they came for our oil, we could never be sure to what extent they would come to influence our government as well.

—MOHAMMED ALMANA
Ibn Saud biographer

Ibn Sa'ūd was pleased to get the concession money, but he did not expect anything further from the oil deal. Engineers and equipment arrived along the Persian Gulf coast, and the slow work of hunting for oil began. In the meantime, affairs on the other side of the Arabian Peninsula occupied the king's attention and drew Prince Faisal into another war.

The Saudi clan had long been on friendly terms with Imam Yahya. He was the ruler of Yemen, the country on the southwest coast of Arabia. In the spring of 1934, however, war broke out between Saudi Arabia and Yemen.

There are two contradictory accounts of why the war started. The Saudis claim that tribes from Yemen were raiding settlements in Asir, which was now part of Saudi Arabia, and that Ibn Sa'ūd attacked Yemen only to protect his own people. The Yemenis claim that Ibn Sa'ūd was greedy to expand his territory and that Yemen was the only part of the Arabian Peninsula the Saudis could attack with-

Shibām, in the Yemeni desert. Many of the town's 500 apartment houses, some 8 stories tall, are 1,000 years old — an example of the advanced engineering skills the Arabs have given the rest of the world through the ages. In 1934 a war between Saudi Arabia and Yemen won the Saudis a large piece of the territory known as the Empty Quarter.

out getting into trouble with the British. The border between Saudi Arabia and Yemen had never been clearly demarcated; for generations Yemeni tribespeople had wandered through the region to graze their herds or carry out raids.

Whatever his motives, Ibn Sa'ūd sent his army south toward Yemen in two columns. The first, under Faisal, marched along the Red Sea coast and captured the city of Hodeida. The second, under Saud, marched across the inland mountains. Three British warships anchored offshore near Hodeida to protect the East Indians who owned businesses in Yemen but were British subjects. Faisal's troops kept good order, however, and there was no looting or violence. Saud had more trouble. His troops, accustomed to marching and fighting on the flat plains of the desert, were not at their best in the steep and rocky gorges of the mountains. The snipers of the hill tribes halted his progress well short of Sana, the capital of Yemen, which was his goal.

Faisal was certain he could take Sana without difficulty, and he was about to begin the attack when he received a message from the king telling him to withdraw. Faisal ignored the telegram and continued his advance, the only time in his life that he would defy his father. But his defiance was short-lived: When a second message arrived, Faisal called a halt.

Saudi legend abounds in speculation about the contents of the king's second message; some versions even have Ibn Sa'ūd threatening to cut off his son's head if he did not obey. No one is sure what it said, but it must have been something very forceful — Ibn Sa'ūd did not tolerate disobedience — and it prompted Faisal to retreat to Hodeida. There he learned that his father and Imam Yahya had agreed on peace terms. The border between the two countries was subsequently marked out officially, and Yemen had to pay Saudi Arabia an amount equal to the cost of the war.

Despite Ibn Sa'ūd's momentary displeasure, Faisal was viewed as a hero for his successes in the Yemen campaign, and upon his return he was greeted with full honors by his father. Faisal's performance also served to point out Saud's lack of success in Yemen. The outcome of the six-week war was a better boundary in the south of the kingdom —and greater dissension between two of its princes.

Faisal (seated center) in his tent with the generals of his forces during the campaign against Yemen in 1934. Though Faisal incurred his father's wrath for not following his orders promptly, he returned a hero for his battlefield successes. The black man standing on the left is Murzouq, Faisal's longtime slave.

The next five years passed fairly quietly for Faisal. He went about his business in Mecca and Jidda, with occasional trips to foreign capitals. But all the while, events elsewhere in the world were coming together in a way that would soon transform Arabia and the Middle East forever.

The first major event was the discovery of oil in eastern Saudi Arabia. The Americans had drilled six holes into a rock formation called Dammam Dome, the place that seemed to be the most likely site for petroleum deposits. Six wells had come up dry. A seventh well was dug, and initially it appeared equally unpromising. But the geologists decided to dig just a little deeper, and in March 1938 their patience was rewarded. Well Seven proved to be the lucky well. The drillers struck oil that flowed freely and fast. Saudi Arabia was in the oil business.

Ibn Sa'ūd paid his first visit to the refinery, called Ras Tanura, as the first tanker load of Saudi oil was leaving the little harbor. He admired the wells, the pipeline, and the drilling equipment. Then he rode back to Riyadh, singing and shouting poetry with his brothers and sons in a half-dozen cars, clutching some of the $1 million he had received from the oil company in celebration of the strike. Immense wealth seemed just over the horizon.

Prince Faisal inspects a Royal Air Force bomber during a visit to Britain in March 1939, six months before the outbreak of World War II. Although it officially remained neutral throughout the war, Saudi Arabia granted special privileges to Britain that, in effect, made the Saudis British allies in a noncombat role.

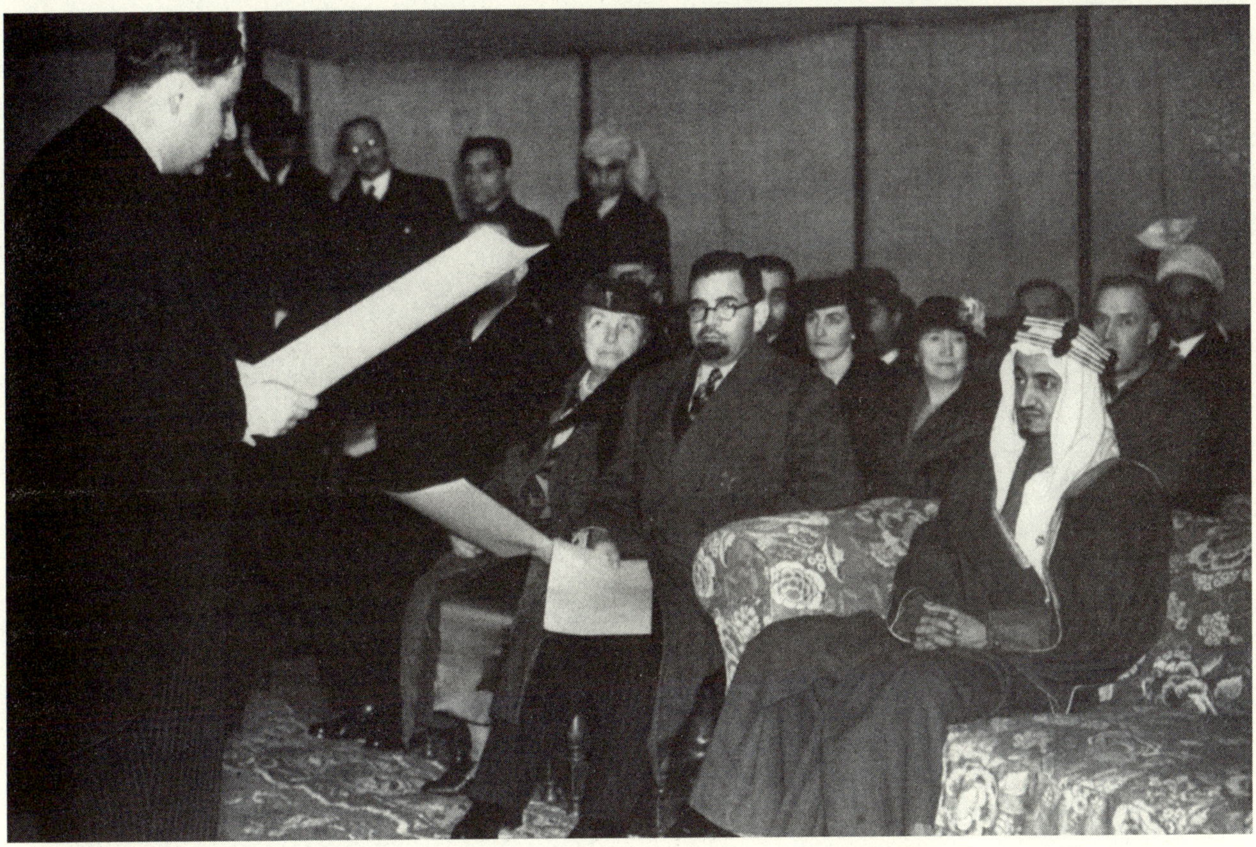

Faisal sits among other Muslim and Jewish dignitaries at the Palestine Conference in London in March 1939. The conclave was called to discuss the future of Palestine, the British-controlled territory populated mostly by Arabs but with an increasing number of Jewish settlers.

But before it could materialize, world events interfered. In September 1939, World War II broke out, and with European and American tankers needed for wartime work, the young Arabian oil industry ground to a halt. The war also affected Saudi Arabia in a second way: the problem of Palestine, where an uneasy relationship between Jews and Arabs had already erupted into fighting on several occasions over the previous decade.

Jewish emigrants from Europe had been settling in Palestine since the late 19th century, viewing their immigration as a return to Zion, their ancestral home. Until they were expelled from Palestine between A.D. 70 and 135 by the Roman Empire, the Jews had lived in Palestine for centuries. The conflict between Arabs and Jews in Palestine began in the late 1800s, with the birth in Europe and Russia of the Zionist movement, which saw the return of Jews from around the world to their ancient homeland in Palestine as a religious, cultural, and moral duty — and as a means to escape the chronic anti-Semitism of Christian society in Europe.

Early Jewish settlers in Palestine. The homeland of the Jews until A.D. 135, when they were expelled by the Roman Empire, the region became the homeland of Palestinian Arabs, most of whom were Muslim. Jewish Zionist settlers, fleeing violent anti-Semitism in Europe, began settling in Palestine during the late 1800s.

When the first Jewish settlers arrived in Palestine, they found the region uncrowded and undeveloped, and many people thought that there was plenty of room for the Jewish newcomers. The Ottoman Turks, who then ruled Palestine as a remote outpost of their huge empire, welcomed the Jews on the grounds that they would help develop the region. By 1900, about 78,000 Jews lived there, making up 1 percent of the Jewish population of the world. But the Arab population of Palestine, about 650,000 strong, was becoming increasingly concerned. The Arabs — who had lived in Palestine for centuries and also thought of it as a holy land — wondered just how many Jews were planning to arrive.

In return for Arab assistance in World War I, when Britain conquered the Ottomans' Middle Eastern lands, the British promised Arab leaders that the former Ottoman colonies would be given their independence. At the same time, however, Britain made another promise: In return for the wartime aid of wealthy and powerful Zionist leaders, Britain assured the Zionists that it would favor the establishment of a Jewish national homeland in Palestine after the war.

It was obvious, of course, that Britain could not possibly keep both promises. As Jewish immigration increased in the 1920s and 1930s, so did Arab resentment. The Jews felt that they had a right to live in the land that had been their ancient home and the birthplace of their faith. The Arabs, on the other hand, felt that the land was theirs, because they had been its sole inhabitants for many centuries before the Zionists arrived. A peaceable solution seemed impossible. Violent incidents, such as bombings and assassinations, became increasingly frequent on both sides; in addition, both the Arabs and the Jews frequently attacked the governing British. In 1933, when Adolf Hitler came to power in Germany and began the full-scale persecution of Jews in that country, pressure to create a formal Jewish homeland in Palestine increased.

Of all Saudi Arabians, Faisal in his role as foreign minister probably had the greatest awareness of events in Palestine and Europe and what they might mean for Arabs everywhere. Early in 1939 he led a delegation of Arabs to an unsuccessful Arab-Jewish conference in London, and he was the only Saudi who was used to thinking in international terms. But once World War II broke out in September of that year, the British had more pressing concerns than that of finding a solution to the problem of Palestine.

Saudi Arabia did not enter the war. Ibn Sa'ūd insisted on remaining neutral, in spite of the efforts of some of his advisers to draw him into the conflict as an ally of Germany. The war caused financial troubles to the Saudi government and hardship to the people because the country's oil income was cut off, and the number of pilgrims to Mecca and Medina decreased sharply. The wily king waited patiently to see which side offered him the greater advantage. When the Germans asked for permission to open an embassy in Jidda, Ibn Sa'ūd granted it. But when the British agreed to help Saudi Arabia by providing wartime aid amounting to $1 million, the Germans were asked to leave. It is probable that Faisal counseled his father to bend his neutrality in the direction of the Allies.

British troops guard against Jewish and Arab rioters in Tel Aviv in 1938. While the British promised Arab leaders that Palestine would be made an independent Arab state after the war, they also promised Jewish leaders that it would be made an independent Jewish state. Arabs and Jews often clashed with each other and with the British.

If so, Faisal was wise. Had Saudi Arabia favored the Germans, it might well have been attacked by the Allied forces. As a neutral friend of the Allies, however, it remained in the good graces of the eventual victors. Even before the war ended, the United States made a gesture of friendship — probably aimed at protecting its claim on the Saudi oil fields. The American government invited Ibn Sa'ūd or any member of his family to visit the United States.

The idea of the visit had originated a year or two before, when an American diplomat in Cairo happened to hear that Prince Saud had expressed a wish to see America. But when the official invitation was received in Riyadh, Ibn Sa'ūd decided that Saud was not to go. Instead, he sent Faisal and his younger brother Khalid (who had been named after the brother who had died in infancy many years before). Although the decision was based on the younger princes' ability to get along with foreigners, it cannot have helped to heal the discord between Saud and Faisal. It pleased Faisal, however, who had already discovered that the good-natured, even-tempered Khalid was his favorite traveling companion.

> ***[Oil production] began in 1938, but fell almost to nothing during the Second World War.***
> —MOHAMMED ALMANA
> Ibn Saud biographer

The princes and their entourage arrived in Miami by airplane and then went on to Washington, D.C., the first stop on their itinerary. They were received by President Franklin D. Roosevelt and honored with a state dinner at the White House. Faisal later met privately with the president. It is not known what the two men discussed, although they must have talked about the growing Arab concern over events in Palestine. But what most concerned them was the U.S. decision, made a few months previously, to provide loans and aid to Saudi Arabia.

The United States had shown no desire to give money to the Saudis until the middle of World War II, when the U.S. government began to fear it was running out of Texas oil, which was being pumped out at the rate of nearly 4 million barrels a day to support the war effort. The feeling quickly grew among statesmen that America should guard its own reserves by cultivating the friendship of nations with oil to spare. One result of this feeling was the prompt approval of a $33 million loan to Saudi Arabia.

After they had completed their visit to Washington, Faisal and Khalid went to New York, where they stayed at the famous Waldorf-Astoria Hotel. Their presence caused something of a dilemma for the hotel management. As always, Faisal was accompanied by Murzouq, his black slave and lifelong bodyguard; Khalid's slave-bodyguard was also in the party. When the royal entourage arrived in the hotel's elegant Wedgewood Room for dinner, Faisal and Khalid expected their slaves to dine with them as they had done since childhood. Fearful of causing an international incident, the hotel agreed — and two Arabian slaves became the first blacks ever permitted to eat in the Wedgewood Room.

While in New York, the princes were like any other tourists, eager to see what the big city had to offer. They visited the top of the Empire State Building, the Stock Exchange, and the Statue of Liberty. Then they took a cross-country train to the West Coast, where they spent a week in both San Francisco and Los Angeles. Their hosts, officials of the Arabian-American Oil Company (Aramco), escorted them to the Petrified Forest National Park in Arizona, the Grand Canyon, and a Hollywood film studio. Returning east, the Arabian party stopped in Detroit, where the princes tried to buy 14 cars for their relatives at home; they were disappointed to learn that, under wartime regulations, only 2 cars could be shipped out of the country.

How can I shake hands with you when you are assisting the Zionists against us?
—IBN SAUD
to President Franklin Roosevelt at their first meeting

They spent another few days in Washington while Faisal and State Department officials ironed out the details of the loan. The prince once again brought up the subject of growing unrest among the Arabs of the Middle East over Zionism in Palestine. Then, although his plans called for him to return to Saudi Arabia, the prince decided to visit England, which was then under almost daily attack by the German air force.

The Arabians arrived in London in November. As they were driven to their hotel through the blacked-out city, they heard the sound of bombs falling not far away. Their escort asked if they would like to be driven to a nearby bomb shelter, but the princes hurriedly agreed that they would put their trust in Allah and stay above ground. They remained unhurt that night and throughout their visit, which included an audience with King George VI at the bomb-damaged Buckingham Palace. A few days later they flew to Gibraltar, then stopped briefly in the North African Arab nations of Algeria, Tunisia, Libya, and Egypt before returning to Riyadh after a three-month absence.

Ibn Sa'ūd himself became interested in meeting Roosevelt and in early 1945 invited him to a meeting at the Suez Canal. The Saudi king and his entourage were taken aboard a U.S. destroyer while Roosevelt arrived on another ship to meet them. It was only the second time the king had left Arabia; the first had been during World War I, when he went to Iraq to see some British army camps.

The meeting between the Saudi king and the U.S. president proved to be something of a culture shock for both Arabs and Americans. The Americans were startled when Ibn Sa'ūd's cook tried to lead 100 live sheep onto their ship, claiming that the king could not eat food from little cans and that he would certainly invite the sailors to a mutton feast every night. Finally, the cook and the ship's captain agreed on seven sheep for the king's use, and the cook promptly set about slaughtering and skinning one on the deck. The sailors were alarmed when the king's coffee servers kindled their open fires in the gun turrets near live ammunition. When the Saudis conducted their five-times-a-day ritual of facing Mecca and praying, the ship's compass was used to determine the precise direction for the prayers.

For their part, the Arabs were interested in the ship's armaments and in other aspects of American culture. They were shown a patriotic documentary film about the war in the Pacific, and Ibn Sa'ūd worried about the possible harmful effects of movies on his people's religious devotion. He would have been far more worried if he had gotten wind of what happened below deck that night; hearing that a Hollywood comedy was being shown to the crew, Prince Muhammad wangled an invitation for himself and his brothers. The Arab princes sat in the front row of the mess hall and watched Lucille Ball scampering around a men's college in her underwear.

On the serious side, the meeting between Roosevelt and Ibn Sa'ūd, with Faisal at his side, betrayed a deeper clash of cultures. The two men talked about Palestine and about the Jews, millions of whom had been killed in Hitler's concentration camps. When Roosevelt asked whether the king agreed that the Jews deserved help, the king's answer was brief and to the point: "Give them the choicest lands of the Germans."

The truth of the matter was simply that the king, like all Arabs, was firmly opposed to the idea of a Jewish nation in Palestine. Roosevelt, on the other hand, had to face the political reality that American Jews strongly supported the creation of the Jewish state. The president felt, however, that Ibn Sa'ūd's viewpoint should be heard, and he agreed to the king's suggestion that a delegation should be sent to the Western nations to explain the Arab point of view.

Roosevelt and Ibn Sa'ūd parted on friendly terms. The king was confident that the American president understood his views on Palestine and would not support the Jews against the Arabs. Faisal, with more knowledge of international diplomacy and political realities, was not so sure.

Ibn Sa'ūd meets with U.S. president Franklin D. Roosevelt aboard a U.S. warship in the Suez Canal in February 1945, toward the end of World War II. Though the two disagreed over the postwar status of Palestine, the meeting helped lay the groundwork for the close future relationship between Saudi Arabia and the United States.

6

The Crown Prince

If you want to be generous, then be generous of what you have.

—FAISAL
addressing the United Nations on the plan to create a Jewish state in Palestine

As World War II drew to a close in 1945, Britain, the United States, the Soviet Union, and their allies were poised on the brink of total victory. In the war's final months, Saudi Arabia declared war on Germany. Though it was purely a formal declaration and involved no military activity, it enabled Saudi Arabia to join the new international organization, the United Nations, as a charter member.

Faisal attended the opening sessions of the UN as his nation's ambassador, again with Khalid for company. The first meeting of the UN was held in San Francisco. During a break between sessions, the two princes were seen in a rare moment of unprincely relaxation, splashing around in small rowboats on a park lake, with their kaffiyehs flying and their robes dripping wet.

Faisal would continue to represent Saudi Arabia at the UN for many years. Before long, he was accepted by many other Arab nations as a general spokesman for the Arab point of view on matters of international concern.

Faisal at the organizing conference of the United Nations in San Francisco in 1945. As Saudi Arabia's UN delegate in subsequent years, Faisal would become the leading spokesman for the Arab cause on Palestine and other issues.

Faisal signs the document making Saudi Arabia a charter member of the UN in 1945. Earlier that year Saudi Arabia also became a charter member of the Arab League, along with Egypt, Iraq, Jordan, Lebanon, Syria, and the Yemen Arab Republic.

After the war ended, the question that most concerned Faisal and other Arab diplomats was: What will happen in Palestine? Faisal knew that once the British withdrew, the Jews would declare statehood. He knew that the United States would not act against the Jews, but he hoped that it would remain neutral. He had received assurances to that effect from American officials.

Harry S. Truman, who had succeeded to the U.S. presidency upon the death of Roosevelt in April 1945, decided that it was impossible to remain neutral. When the State of Israel announced its formation in May 1948, Truman extended official diplomatic recognition to the new nation within 12 minutes. Faisal, furious and humiliated, believed that he had been misled and betrayed by the U.S. government, and he knew that the other Arab delegations felt that he had let them down. Having been booed and spat upon by Zionist demonstrators outside the UN building in New York, he was furious at the Zionists as well.

Faisal did not turn against the United States, like Egypt's president Gamal Abdel Nasser and some other Arab leaders, but he became distrustful of its promises and resolved to maintain his country's independence from the United States in the future. Although the two nations were bound for many years by oil development and by shared opposition to communism, Faisal always treated the U.S. government as a useful tool and never as a friend. Along with most other Saudis and Arabs everywhere, he believed that Israel would not exist today if the United States had had as many Arab voters as Jewish ones.

With the end of World War II in September 1945, oil production resumed at Ras Tanura and at other drilling and refining sites in the area of Dhahran, a city in eastern Saudi Arabia that became the center of the Saudi oil industry. Because no Saudis possessed the technical skills or experience to work in the refineries, Aramco brought in most of its workers from the United States, along with some other non-Saudi Arabs who had experience in technical jobs. Aramco built a large town for the workers and their families. It was like a country within a country, with rows of streets and houses just like the new suburbs that were springing up all over postwar America, right down to the high schools, baseball fields, and even the streetlights.

Drilling, refining, and shipping went on night and day. The revenues generated by the oil industry brought undreamed-of wealth to the Saudis, but it also brought problems. The royal family and government officials who were paid by Aramco prospered, but the common people suffered because the new wealth caused prices to go up all over the country. Part of the problem was Ibn Sa'ūd's attitude toward money.

Decades ago, as the conqueror of Riyadh, he had formed the habit of turning all his funds — in gold and silver coins — over to Abdullah Suleiman, who kept the royal treasury in a chest under his bed and handed out sums whenever Ibn Sa'ūd asked for them. Now that the wealth of his treasury had increased many times, Ibn Sa'ūd could not understand that the same simple system no longer worked. He regarded Saudi Arabia's earnings as his own personal funds, to be handled as he pleased.

A British soldier is hoisted on the shoulders of celebrating Jews after the announcement that the UN would partition Palestine into separate Jewish and Arab states. Violence between Jews and Arabs followed immediately, with each side blaming the other for the bloodshed.

Saudi soldiers in 1948 prepare to leave for the war against Israel. The Arab League nations declared war against the newly independent Jewish state but were defeated and lost more territory. The 1947 partition and 1948 defeat created a large population of Palestinian Arab refugees in Jordan, Lebanon, and Egypt.

And what pleased him was to continue his old customs: entertaining lavishly, giving generously to anyone who asked for help or a favor, and showering presents on his family and friends.

Before long, however, the old king grew troubled by some of the consequences of the new wealth. He saw that some of his children and grandchildren were greatly attracted to material possessions and Western ways; some of them even drank alcohol, which was forbidden by the Koran. Ibn Sa'ūd also realized that luxuries such as automobiles, telephones, and record players, which he had enjoyed as novelties and toys, were now changing the face of Arabia forever. The simple desert life, with its uncomplicated routine of prayer and work and its lack of concern for the outside world, was vanishing.

These concerns darkened the final years of the man who had built Saudi Arabia. Toward the end of his life, in the late 1940s and early 1950s, Ibn Sa'ūd was in poor health and often melancholy, wondering if the path upon which he had set his people would lead to a breakdown of faith and order. He turned over most of the administration of the kingdom to Saud, Faisal, and others of his family. Everyone knew that a successor to the Saudi throne would soon have to be chosen.

The succession of kingship in the Saudi royal family is not a straightforward matter of passing the throne to the oldest son. Over the centuries, the Saudis had formed a meritocracy, or a system of rule by merit. The power of government was given to the family members who were agreed to be best qualified to rule well. Thus 'Abd ar-Rahmān had recognized the leadership qualities of his son Ibn Sa'ūd and turned over the chieftainship of the clan to him. And Ibn Sa'ūd had held off from naming Saud as his heir until Saud had earned respect in the family by quelling the Ikhwan rebellion.

Nevertheless, the old king knew that Faisal possessed skills and qualities that in some ways outshone those of Saud. He also knew that the two brothers had not always gotten along, although Faisal scrupulously followed the Arab custom of respect for senior members of the family and never publicly disagreed with Saud. Ibn Sa'ūd wanted the brothers to work together after his death.

In 1953, as he felt death drawing near, he had Saud and Faisal brought to his bedside. He made them join hands over his bed and swear an oath that they would not quarrel. He told Faisal to accept Saud as king after his death, and he told Saud to appoint Faisal as his crown prince. When the king died in his sleep on November 9, 1953, his sons carried out his wishes. Saud became king of Saudia Arabia, and Faisal, still foreign minister, was named as his heir.

By this time, the two brothers were quite different. Saud had lived most of his life in Nejd, where he liked to stay with the desert tribes. He duplicated many of his father's ways, especially his irresponsibility with money and his fondness for the harem. To many Saudi Arabians, Saud stood for the old way of life. Those who wished to preserve this way of life favored Saud.

Faisal, on the other hand, was both more pious and more sophisticated than Saud. His personal life was austere and quite religious, but he also had a reputation for being learned and cosmopolitan; he was known for traveling abroad and experiencing other cultures. In addition, he had lived for decades in Hejaz, which many Nedjis still regarded as a somewhat foreign place. Those Saudi Arabians who were interested in the outside world and who favored modernization and progress tended to favor Faisal.

Saud and two of his bodyguards. King Ibn Sa'ūd died in November 1953, having designated Prince Saud to be his successor; he had also ordered Saud to appoint Faisal as crown prince and heir to the throne.

At first the two brothers seemed to get along well enough. Soon, however, problems arose, both within the family and in the realm of international affairs. Saud spent money lavishly, building a whole street of new palaces for himself and his sons, and he began to act against Faisal's advice in foreign affairs.

Saud was especially troubled by the rise to prominence in the Arab world of Egypt's president Nasser, who was supported by the Soviet Union. Nasser was vehemently opposed to the existence of Israel and had seized the Suez Canal from the British and French. These acts made Nasser a hero in Egypt and throughout the Arab world, and Saud did not want to be outdone in popularity among his own people.

The new king went to the United States and managed to obtain armaments and a huge loan in exchange for a promise to oppose communism in the Middle East. Faisal had counseled against such a move, feeling that it would tie Saudi Arabia too closely to U.S. policy. But Faisal was laid up in a different part of America, undergoing operations to remove his gall bladder and a tumor. Saud ignored his brother's advice.

In view of all the oil money the kingdom was earning, it seemed odd to some that Saud would need a $180 million loan from the U.S. government. But the Americans were willing to pay out whatever was necessary to preserve their oil interests and to secure an anticommunist ally in the Middle East, and Saud knew it. Without consulting his family, the new king spent much of the money on a bribe of several million dollars made to a Syrian official in order to sabotage a planned union between Egypt and Syria. Keeping Syria out of Nasser's camp was exactly what both Saud and the U.S. government wanted, but when the bribe payment was exposed, it caused great embarrassment to the Saudi government.

The Ras Tanura refinery in 1948. Oil was first struck in Saudi Arabia in 1938 and exported a year later. Production slowed during World War II but increased greatly after the war. Until the advent of oil, the Saudi government's primary sources of revenue were an annual tax levied on Saudi citizens and fees paid by pilgrims to the holy cities.

King Saud with Syrian president Shukri al-Kuwatli (left) and Egyptian president Gamal Abdel Nasser in 1956. That year, Nasser nationalized the Suez Canal, prompting a British- and French-backed invasion of Egypt by Israel. Nasser, a socialist, was a hero to much of the Arab world for his leadership in asserting Arab nations' rights.

Saud caused further domestic disruption by ignoring the custom of meritocracy, which had always been a part of Saudi clan life. He removed from office many of his uncles and brothers, as well as other officials who had served under Ibn Sa'ūd, and replaced them with his own sons. More and more he turned to his sons and to new followers to help him make decisions, shutting out his uncles, brothers, and other proved advisers. Members of the family started to worry that Saud wanted to turn the kingship into a personal dynasty instead of a family one.

By 1958, the kingdom faced a crisis. Saud had spent $200 million on new government ministry buildings in Riyadh and millions more on his family, and the kingdom was bankrupt. Civil servants and soldiers had not been paid in months. Many senior members of the Saudi clan had lost confidence in Saud's leadership.

In March, nine of King Saud's brothers gathered to discuss the state of affairs. Faisal was not among them; he had remained aloof from all discussion of Saud's shortcomings, either as a clever political maneuver or out of the sense that it was not his place to criticize his sovereign, or perhaps both. The brothers, meanwhile, told Saud that most family members felt that Faisal should take over the day-to-day running of the government. He had more than 30 years of experience as an administrator, and he was known to be fair-minded, honest, and hardworking.

The family persuaded Saud to turn the executive, or decision-making, power of government over to Faisal, although Saud kept the title of king. Faisal agreed to accept the responsibility of government. His first task was to straighten out Saudi Arabia's finances. He obtained short-term loans to cover the back pay of government employees, and he made some strict new budgets to get the kingdom back in good financial shape.

One of these budgets involved royal spending. Previously, whenever a member of the House of Saud wanted money, he would simply go to the royal treasurer and get it. Now Faisal put each member of the family on a fixed monthly pension. He began paying back the costly interest on some of Saudi Arabia's foreign loans. He also postponed some of Saud's ambitious building and development plans until he had the money to pay for them.

> ***The oil brings money. But in many ways it is a burden to me.***
> —IBN SAUD

Before long, Faisal had the kingdom on the road to fiscal recovery. He then turned his attention to the oil business, believing that Saudi Arabia needed to make the most profit possible from this, its only resource. Up until now, the oil companies had set the price of oil themselves, paying Saudi Arabia a certain percentage of the price for each barrel sold. But Faisal was beginning to believe that the oil could be sold more profitably. With this in mind, he listened to a plan urged by the country's oil minister, Abdullah al-Tariki, who thought that the oil-producing nations should unite in negotiating with the foreign oil companies to force up the price of crude oil on the world market. The higher prices would mean more money for the oil-producing countries. Thus, in 1960, Faisal approved al-Tariki's plan to form OPEC, the Organization of Petroleum Exporting Countries. Although OPEC was not powerful enough to challenge the oil companies right away, its formation set the stage for later petroleum politics.

Approving Saudi Arabia's membership in OPEC was Faisal's last act as head of the government in 1960. Saud was growing anxious to have the reins of power in his own hands again, and some of the family members who had previously supported Saud's removal had grown tired of Faisal's tight control of the purse strings. Later that year, Saud reclaimed his powers and Faisal agreed to return to his post as foreign minister. But by late 1961, Saud was suffering from eye trouble, liver trouble, and stomach ulcers. Too ill to govern, he withdrew to Europe and the United States for medical treatment, and in 1962 Faisal once again took executive control of Saudi Arabia.

Upon regaining power, Faisal removed al-Tariki, who had become too outspoken and powerful and was accused of taking bribes. He appointed a new oil minister, Sheik Adman Zaki Yamani, who would remain in the post throughout the turbulent years of OPEC's rise to world prominence in the early 1970s.

At first, though, Faisal's biggest challenge was in Yemen. In September 1962, Nasser ordered Egyptian troops to invade Yemen and help local revolutionaries overthrow the royal family. Relations between procommunist Egypt and anticommunist Saudi Arabia, already poor, had deteriorated further because of Saud's blundering attempt to cause trou-

A typically American suburban subdivision, but one located in 'Udhailiyah, Saudi Arabia. Several such self-contained towns were built for the thousands of American workers employed by Aramco (the Arabian-American Oil Company) under an arrangement with the Saudi government to keep foreigners separate from the Saudi population.

ble between Egypt and Syria. Now the Egyptian invasion of Yemen was an invitation to open war.

Faisal thought that Nasser would try to conquer Saudi Arabia and its oil fields if war was declared, but he also believed that a war with Egypt would be far too destructive and expensive, even if Saudi Arabia prevailed. He decided not to commit Saudi troops to Yemen, but rather sent financial aid to the royalists there, fighters who opposed the Eygptians and the revolutionaries. It was a wise move: Guerrilla warfare in Yemen would continue until 1972, with heavy losses to Egyptian forces. The cost to the Saudis was merely in terms of money.

In 1964, King Saud returned from his overseas treatments to Nasriyah Palace outside Riyadh and ordered the 1,500 men of the Royal Guard to patrol its 7-mile-long wall with loaded rifles. The smoke of their campfires made black stains on the pink-painted wall, and each day they seemed more menacing. Saud's sons holed up in the palace with their father. It seemed clear that Saud was planning to seize full control of the government, and this time the rest of the clan was united against him. Only Faisal, mindful of the profound respect he owed Saud as his elder and his king, stayed away from the agitated family councils. He retreated to the desert to rest and hunt.

Under pressure from family members, Saud finally emerged from his palace and signed an agreement to leave executive power in Faisal's hands. A few months later, however, he reversed himself and demanded the return of all his powers. He refused to continue as king in name only. In response, the family took drastic action.

If Saud would not be content to reign as king in name only, the Saudis decided, then he could no longer be king. With the support of the religious leaders of the ulema, the Saudi clan gathered in October 1964 and formally deposed King Saud. Faisal, who was still in retreat at al-Kharj oasis, was named king. When a delegation of princes carried the news to Faisal, he wept for the shame and distress of his brother and his family. Then he accepted the throne — and, with it, the responsibility thrust upon him by his family.

Saud's mismanagement of the government, the discovery that he had offered millions of dollars for the assassination of Nasser, and what the Muslim clergy viewed as Saud's personal impiety caused his formal ouster as monarch in October 1964. The Saudi family and the ulema named Faisal the new king.

7

King Faisal

Faisal is perhaps the last big hope in Saudi Arabia.
—*The Scotsman*
an Edinburgh newspaper

With the consent of the family, King Faisal appointed his brother, Khalid, crown prince. Muhammad, the brother who was next to Faisal in seniority, did not wish to be king and gave up his succession. Khalid was a good choice. Not only had he earned diplomatic and administrative skills by traveling and working with Faisal, but he was known within the family as good-natured and friendly to all — just the prince to heal the tensions that Saud's kingship and deposition had caused.

As soon as Faisal assumed the throne, he set about a wide-ranging program of reforms to which he must have given much thought in the preceding years. He wanted to make the best use of Saudi Arabia's oil wealth for the benefit of all the people, not just the royal family. He also wanted to become independent of the foreign governments and oil companies that provided skilled labor and other services to the kingdom. And he knew, as many Saudis did not, that there was no place in the modern world for a country that refused to be part of the international community.

As head of the day-to-day operations of the government during Saud's reign, Faisal had instituted several modernization programs, which he accelerated upon becoming king in 1964. During the 11 years of his reign he presided over one of the greatest economic booms any nation has ever experienced.

Saudi schoolboys in class in the 1950s, part of Faisal's push for education. By the end of his reign, enough schools had been built to accommodate nearly 1 million students. Nearly a third of the students were female — a marked departure from Saudis' traditional disdain for educating women.

In order for Saudi Arabia to take its place in the world, however, the country would have to change in some ways. King Faisal's task was to allow change to happen in ways that did not threaten or destroy the important values of his country, such as its religion and its traditional male-dominated family structure.

Faisal knew that education in the kingdom would have to become more modern and more universal. He also felt that some innovations that were resisted by the ulema, such as television, could be used to the people's benefit without corrupting them. With the help of his wife, Iffat, he waged many subtle campaigns to get his way.

Iffat's contribution was her interest in education for women. She had grown up in Turkey, where women had slightly greater freedom and opportunities than in many Muslim lands. She convinced Faisal that education for girls would not threaten Saudi society, and he allowed her to open the first girls' schools in Saudi Arabia. In order to avoid protests by outraged elders of the ulema, however, the schools were initially called clubs. Attendance was small, but it grew over the years. Gradually, the idea of education for women gained some acceptance, largely due to Iffat's influence with the Saudi family and the people at large. Today, girls in Saudi Arabia are not required to attend school the way boys are, but they are not prevented from attending if they choose to do so. Many young women have attended college and medical school with the help of scholarships from Iffat.

A bedouin family in the desert oil fields. Faisal pushed forward his father's plan to end the traditional nomadic way of life of Saudi Arabia's large bedouin population. With oil accounting for 99 percent of the nation's exports, Faisal hoped to train the bedouin as industrial workers.

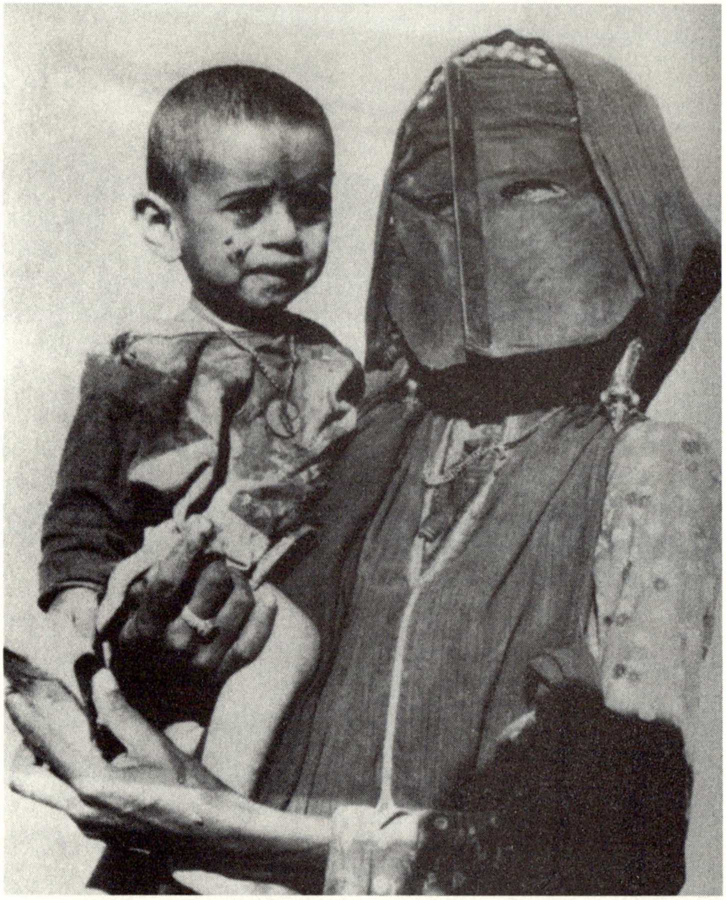

A southern Arabian tribeswoman, her face hidden by a canvas mask in a local interpretation of general Islamic custom. Women's roles in traditional Arabian society have been strictly limited to those of wife and mother, and men have as many as four wives at a time. Thus Ibn Sa'ūd and Saud each had more than 100 children; Faisal had 14.

Another area in which Faisal had to move cautiously at first was television. Ibn Sa'ūd had talked the ulema into allowing the telephone and the radio into Arabia in the 1920s, and many old holy men still resented these Western devices; the strictest members of the ulema thought they were the work of Satan. So, in order to make television available for news and educational shows, Faisal introduced it as a religious tool, with a program of nonstop prayer and Koran readings. Resistance continued, however, and it took a tragic turn.

Prince Khalid ibn Musa'id, one of the sons of Faisal's brother Musa'id, was the leader of a group of ultrastrict young Muslims, not unlike the earlier Wahhabis and Ikhwan. Ironically, Khalid had been one of the more dissipated younger princes until, during a drunken orgy on a Paris rooftop, he claimed to have experienced a religious vision and thenceforth devoted himself to strict religious observance.

In Riyadh, he and his fellow zealots opposed the introduction of television and decided to take matters into their own hands. Led by Khalid, they mounted an armed attack on the new television studio. The chief of Faisal's security forces called the king and asked what he should do — the idea of shedding a prince's blood was unthinkable. "None of us is above the law," Faisal told him. "If the prince fires at you, then you must fire back." In the ensuing battle, Prince Khalid was shot through the head and killed. Thereafter, Faisal proceeded to add news and educational shows to the religious television programs, an hour or two at a time.

Another milestone in Faisal's reign was a summit conference of Islamic nations that he organized in Rabat, the capital of Morocco, in 1967. It was the first formal gathering of Muslim heads of state from around the world, and it was the result of long planning by King Faisal. As early as 1956, Faisal had dreamed of a pan-Islamic federation, an organization of all Islamic peoples from Africa, the Middle East, India, and Southeast Asia. In 1964, he started trying to interest his fellow heads of state in the idea, but made little progress.

New York demonstrators in 1957, during a visit by King Saud, protest the existence of slavery in Saudi Arabia. King Faisal abolished the age-old institution in 1962 and had the government compensate former slave-owners $2,000 for each of the 1,682 slaves freed.

After the Six-Day War in June of 1967, when Israel won control of Egyptian, Jordanian, and Syrian territory, the Muslim leaders of the world agreed to come together at Faisal's invitation. They were particularly outraged that, soon after the Israelis seized control of the Old City of Jerusalem, a fire had started in the ancient Asqa Mosque there. When 25 Islamic kings, sultans, and presidents met in Rabat, they united in condemnation of Israel. The conference resulted in the formation of a permanent worldwide Islamic organization that included a bank and a news agency. Faisal's dream of a pan-Islamic federation did not come true in entirety, but he did more to bring Muslim states together than any other modern leader.

Meanwhile, Saud was living out his final years in exile, first in Beirut, then in Cairo, and finally in Athens and the Greek islands, where he surprised diners on hotel terraces by offering them $1,000 to

Muslim pilgrims to Mecca read the Koran. Though Faisal was a devout Wahhabi Muslim, his reforms were considered sacrilegious by many in the ulema and in the general population. In the mid-1960s, the introduction of television sparked a short-lived rebellion by one of Faisal's nephews.

A meeting of OPEC (the Organization of Petroleum Exporting Countries). Founded in 1960, its members are the Arab states of Saudi Arabia, Iraq, Kuwait, Libya, Algeria, Qatar, and the United Arab Emirates; the non-Arab but largely Islamic states of Iran, Nigeria, and Indonesia; and Venezuela and Gabon.

dive, fully dressed, into the sea. His living expenses — including Ferraris for his sons to demolish, banquets brought from distant restaurants in chauffeured limousines, and other extravagances — were enormous. In 1968, he spent $10 million, a full 1 percent of Greece's total foreign currency income for the year.

But despite his lavish life-style, Saud was unhappy and ill. He died in February 1969, and Faisal sent a plane to bring his body back to Riyadh for burial.

At about the same time, Faisal introduced Saudi Arabia's first five-year plan, outlining the proposed economic development for the coming half decade. The plan, which spelled out Faisal's thoughts on loan repayments, construction projects, and other administrative details, was the first formal program the government had ever had. It was the beginning of a new, organized, systematic approach to growth and spending.

In the middle of the five-year period covered by the plan, Faisal agreed with Yamani, his oil minister, that the time had come for OPEC to start wielding its power against the oil companies. For a long time, the companies had set oil prices; then, in the late 1960s, the companies and OPEC had negotiated a small price increase. Now Yamani and Faisal and the member nations of OPEC were ready to demand a large increase, whether the oil companies agreed or not. If the oil companies refused to meet the new price, oil production would be shut down, the foreigners would be expelled, and the OPEC nations would attempt to run the industry alone.

During the very week that the OPEC ministers were negotiating with oil company representatives in Vienna, Austria, the 1973 October War broke out. Faisal's reaction was to stop all oil shipments to Israel's supporters, but the excitement aroused by this oil embargo almost obscured the fact that for the first time the OPEC nations had forced the oil companies to accept a unilateral, or one-sided, price increase. The price of oil jumped from $3.01 to $5.12 per barrel, and a few weeks later it was raised again, to $11.65.

The OPEC nations had discovered their power. The world needed oil, and they could charge as much for it as the traffic would bear. The oil companies had no choice but to cooperate, or they would be left out of the industry entirely — and they stood to make enormous profits because of the OPEC price hikes. By 1981, oil had reached $32 per barrel, a 1,000-percent increase over the pre-hike price of $3.01. Saudi Arabia was selling 10 million barrels a day, which gave the country a daily income of $320 million. Although prices would decline somewhat in subsequent years, they would never again return to the low levels of the years prior to 1973.

Saudi oil minister Ahmed Zaki Yamani, who with Faisal engineered the OPEC price hikes of 1973–74 in response to the October War between Israel and its Arab neighbors. Nevertheless, other OPEC officials and member nations wanted still higher prices than those advocated by Faisal and Yamani.

A second Islamic summit conference was held in Pakistan in 1974. Like the 1967 conference, it resulted in a condemnation of Israel. It differed from the 1967 conference, however, in welcoming a delegation from the Palestine Liberation Organization (PLO), a political and military organization representing Palestinian Arabs. The PLO had been carrying on a guerrilla war against Israel for decades, and Faisal believed it was his duty as an Arab head of state to aid the organization. Saudi Arabia promised to support Yasir Arafat, the head of the PLO, with a substantial monthly cash payment well into the 1990s.

Faisal with Muhammad Reza Pahlavi, the Shah of Iran. These two monarchs of oil-rich Muslim nations were the United States' closest allies in the Middle East outside of Israel. The United States sold huge amounts of arms to both Saudi Arabia and Iran. Yet in the 1970s the shah pressed for still higher oil price hikes, a move headed off by Faisal.

The October War and the events that followed it had one further consequence: On the heels of the tremendous flood of oil money that flowed into the kingdom, there was an unprecedented boom in the Saudi economy. Financiers and businessmen descended upon Saudi Arabia from all over the world, each with something to sell or some new scheme to peddle. The Saudi princes and the wealthy merchants of Riyadh and other cities were delighted. Car imports tripled. Property values in Riyadh doubled every week. At every moment, it seemed, everyone was making money.

8

Royal Murder

> ***One of the most inextricable crimes of the last half century cut short the life of a King unanimously admired, loved and venerated in his country.***
> —MARCEL GROS
> Faisal biographer

The hallmarks of King Faisal's reign were order and punctuality. Every day he followed the same routine, and every hour had its special task. He rose at dawn to make the first prayer of the day, kneeling in the courtyard of his private palace among his family, servants, and guests; there were always guests at the palace, usually bedouin visiting from the desert who claimed hospitality from their leader, according to ancient tribal customs. He then went into town to the government palace, where he received visitors in his majlis, or council room, between 9:00 and 10:00 A.M. At 10:00 he would go to his office and work there for the rest of the morning.

He returned to his palace for the midday prayer and lunch in the company of whichever advisers and guests presented themselves. Afterward, he rested for half an hour, made the afternoon prayer, and went back to his office. At sunset each day he drove out into the desert, where he would meet various brothers, sons, uncles, and old friends for the evening prayer and a session of gossip or reminiscence. The king ate dinner at his palace, once again in public company; Iffat and his younger children ate a separate meal.

King Faisal in prayer. By the mid-1970s oil had made Saudi Arabia one of the world's wealthiest nations; in 1974 alone, the Saudi government made $30 billion on oil exports. Faisal used the money to modernize Saudi Arabia and to extend aid to other Muslim nations.

The Grand Mosque during the annual pilgrimage period that draws as many as 2 million Muslims to Mecca from around the world. Despite its wealth, Saudi Arabia still strictly adheres to Koranic law.

At 9:00 P.M., Faisal went back to the office to work until 11:30. When he returned home, however, his day was still not over. His closest advisers and governors met with him around midnight and usually stayed for about an hour, reporting on their activities and hearing his opinions. Sometimes they all listened to radio broadcasts from various Middle Eastern capitals.

The king also encouraged his sons to express themselves at these late-night councils, urging them to debate the strengths and weaknesses of various points of view. Abdullah, the oldest, was a middle-aged poet and businessman who had served as minister of the interior from 1953 to 1960. The seven younger sons were educated in England and the United States, and some of them were still completing their schooling. They went on to play their roles in the family-run government of Saudi Arabia: Muhammad became president of the Islamic Bank, which had been founded by his father; Khalid served as governor of Asir; Saud became foreign minister; Abdul Rahman served in the armed forces; Sa'ūd was a deputy governor; Bandar served in the Royal Saudi Air Force and the ministry of defense; and Turkī became director of foreign intelligence.

During Faisal's reign, Saudi Arabia became known to the rest of the world as a land of startling contrasts. Immense wealth existed side by side with a strict moral and religious code. Sometimes the two appeared to be compatible. The hundreds of new computers that were brought into the kingdom, for example, were specially programmed so that each printout began "In the name of Allah."

Other adjustments did not come so easily. Princes jetted and yachted around the world with great sophistication, yet some aspects of life in the kingdom seemed medieval and were difficult to reconcile with the ways of the outside world. Thieves were punished by having their hands cut off. Graver offenses were punishable by public beheading — in the early 1980s, in fact, a Saudi princess was beheaded in Riyadh after being convicted of adultery. And slavery had existed in the kingdom until Faisal abolished it in 1962. Slaves in Saudi Arabia were few in number and were almost always regarded as family or clan members, but the Saudis resisted the abolition of slavery until Faisal insisted upon it. After the slaves were freed, however, most of them remained with the families that had owned them; they showed no desire to seek out other ways of life.

Desert travelers bow toward Mecca during one of five daily prayer periods observed by devout Muslims. In 1974 alone, Faisal directed $200 million in aid to Egypt, Jordan, and Syria, and $800 million to other Muslim nations without oil resources, as part of a total of $3 billion in foreign-aid programs.

As the years passed, Faisal began to have misgivings about his country's future. He feared that petrodollars and jet setting would erode traditional Arab values. Like his father before him, he viewed the increasing Westernization of the younger generation and wondered where it would end. Faisal had been raised by his grandfather, a strict Wahhabi, and now he began to fear that, in his zeal to improve the life of his people, he had betrayed them into a future of materialism.

By about 1974, Faisal's friends and family noticed his increasing melancholy and remoteness. He worked harder and harder, yet seemed less and less satisfied with what he had done for Saudi Arabia. At the same time, his health worsened. Faisal had never been one of the more robust members of his family, and he had suffered from several serious illnesses as an adult. In addition, he had always been one of the hardest-working Saudis and had carried a heavy burden of responsibility since his first official mission at age 14.

Faisal, wearing the white robe of a Muslim pilgrim, praying in Mecca. Faisal was an accessible king who, despite his full schedule, would listen at length to even the poorest of his subjects. In the last year of his life he often complained of fatigue.

On March 24, 1975, Prince Faisal ibn Musa'id (pictured here), one of King Faisal's nephews, walked into the king's office, pulled out a gun, and fatally wounded him. He gave no explanation for his crime and was publicly beheaded a few months later.

Now, as he approached 70, he lost weight and slept poorly. He confided to a sister that he had dreamed of seeing Ibn Sa'ūd and Tarfah, his mother, who had died when he was a baby. He felt that these dreams were premonitions of coming death. When invited by his son Abdullah to spend a weekend resting at Abdullah's country home, the king replied, "I would be thinking of work all the time. I cannot relax. I can no longer feel for life itself. I tell you, Abdullah, I can no longer tell the difference between what is cold and what is hot."

Perhaps King Faisal would have cast off his growing depression, forgotten his ominous dreams, and ruled for many more productive years; perhaps not. As it happened, his rule and his life were ended suddenly in March 1975.

Faisal ibn Musa'id, one of the king's nephews, was an example of the poor adjustment made by some of the younger Saudis to the challenges and opportunities of wealth and Westernization. Sent to college in the United States, he got into trouble several

Faisal was succeeded as king by his half brother Khalid, who continued Faisal's modernization and foreign-aid programs.

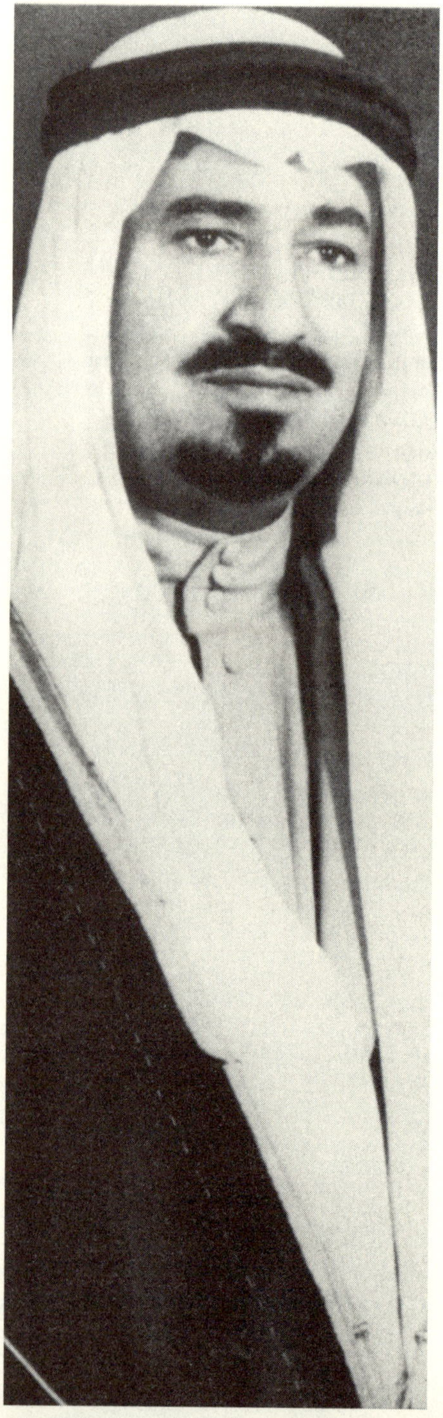

times for brawling and for possessing drugs; only the intervention of the U.S. State Department kept him out of jail. The king felt that his behavior had disgraced the family and ordered him to remain at home for a while. Even in Riyadh, however, the 26-year-old prince led as dissolute a life as possible, drinking whiskey every night with his brothers and friends. These binges usually ended in a long sleep and hangover. But the drinking bout that young Faisal started on the night of March 24 ended differently.

He showed up about 10:00 the next morning at the office of his uncle, the king. As King Faisal reached forward to embrace and kiss his nephew in the traditional Arab greeting, the young man pulled a pistol from beneath his robe and shot his uncle three times. King Faisal died within the hour.

No one knows why Faisal ibn Musa'id assassinated his uncle. It did not appear to have been a political killing or the work of a conspiracy. Perhaps the young prince was angry because he had been detained inside the kingdom; or maybe he intended to avenge the death of his brother Khalid, who had been killed during the television riots. Whatever his motive, the result was the same: Faisal was dead.

Faisal was buried in a humble grave on the outskirts of Riyadh. A few months later his nephew was publicly beheaded.

Faisal was succeeded as king by his brother Khalid, who reigned until 1982, when he died of a heart attack. Khalid was followed by his half brother Fahd, who ruled for the rest of the decade. Like Faisal before them, both Khalid and Fahd presided over the continuing modernization and enrichment of their nation while preserving its traditional cultural values.

Saudi Arabia had come a long way since the childhood of Faisal, whose importance will long be remembered both within his kingdom and outside it. He had been born when a united Arabia was nothing more than a dream in his father's heart. For better or worse, Ibn Sa'ūd had made the dream a reality, and Faisal had witnessed and played a part in the drama of the birth of the kingdom and the discovery of oil.

Ibn Sa'ūd lived to see Arabia united into a single kingdom, but Faisal brought it out of the past and made it into a modern nation, blending progress and tradition to the best of his ability. By using oil as a political tool, he made the Arab voice loud and forceful enough to be heard around the world. He brought a measure of unity to the many different nations living under the Islamic faith. And without his firm leadership, Saudi Arabia might very well have gone bankrupt or fallen victim to revolution, civil war, or invasion.

Today, Saudi Arabia owns one-fourth of the world's known petroleum deposits. In his 11 years as king, Faysal ibn 'Abd al-Azīz ibn 'Abd ar-Rahmān āl-Sa'ūd demonstrated to his countrymen and to the world the power of that resource. But his legacy is more than petropower and petrodollars. It is the example of duty, honor, faith, and principle — even in the face of tremendous temptation — that he hoped to set for Arabs everywhere.

Mourners visit Faisal's grave on the outskirts of Riyadh. While many members of the Saudi family used their wealth to maintain an ostentatious life-style, Faisal remained simple and devout, a choice reflected in the simplicity of his grave.

Further Reading

Alireza, Marianne. *At the Drop of a Veil.* Boston: Houghton Mifflin, 1971.

Almana, Mohammed. *Arabia Unified: A Portrait of Ibn Saud.* London: Hutchinson Benham, 1980.

Beling, Willard A., ed. *King Faisal and the Modernization of Sa'udi Arabia.* London: Croom Helm, 1980.

Bidwell, Robin. *Travellers in Arabia.* London: Hamlyn, 1976.

Blandford, Linda. *Oil Sheikhs.* London: Weidenfeld & Nicholson, 1976.

Bulliet, Richard. *The Camel and the Wheel.* Cambridge, MA: Harvard University Press, 1975.

Clements, Frank A. *Saudi Arabia.* Oxford, England: Clio Press, 1979.

De Gaury, Gerald. *Faisal: King of Saudi Arabia.* New York: Praeger, 1967.

Gordon, Eugene. *Saudi Arabia in Pictures.* New York: Sterling, 1976.

Helms, Christine. *The Cohesion of Saudi Arabia.* London: Croom Helm, 1980.

Hobday, Peter. *Saudi Arabia Today.* London: Macmillan, 1978.

Knauerhase, Ramon. *The Saudi Arabian Economy.* New York: Praeger, 1977.

Lacey, Robert. *The Kingdom: Arabia and the House of Sa'ud.* New York: Harcourt Brace Jovanovich, 1981.

Lamb, David. *The Arabs.* New York: Random House, 1987.

Mackey, Sandra. *The Saudis: Inside the Desert Kingdom.* New York: Houghton Mifflin, 1987.

Mosley, Leonard. *Power Play: Oil in the Middle East.* New York: Random House, 1973.

Raban, Jonathan. *Arabia through the Looking Glass.* London: Collins, 1979.

Sheehan, Vincent. *Faisal: The King and His Kingdom.* Tavistock, England: University Press of Arabia, 1975.

Stegner, Wallace. *Discovery: The Search for Arabian Oil.* Beirut: Middle East Export Press, 1971.

Troeller, Gary. *The Birth of Sa'udi Arabia: Britain and the Rise of the House of Sa'ud.* London: Frank Cass, 1976.

Chronology

1905	Faisal born Faysal ibn 'Abd al-'Azīz in Riyadh to 'Abd al-'Azīz ibn Sa'ūd, ruler of Nejd, and his second wife, Tarfah
1919	Visits India, England, and Europe as his father's official representative
1926	Appointed viceroy (governor) of newly conquered Hejaz district and his father's foreign minister
1932	Founding of the Kingdom of Saudi Arabia; Faisal visits Europe as the new nation's first official ambassador; meets and marries Iffat al-Thunayan
1934	Leads successful military campaign as general in war against Yemen
1939–45	Saudi Arabia sides with Britain and United States as noncombatant in World War II
1946	Marked increase in Saudi Arabian oil production
1953	King Ibn Sa'ūd dies; Faisal's older brother, Saud, becomes king; Faisal is named crown prince
1958	King Saud turns over executive power to Faisal, who imposes financial reforms on his family
1960	Saud reclaims all executive power; Faisal returns to service as foreign minister; Saudi Arabia becomes one of five founding members of OPEC
1962	Saud returns executive power to Faisal; Faisal abolishes slavery
1964	Saud demands the restoration of all powers and is deposed; Faisal becomes king
1967	Saudi Arabia supports the Arab states in Six-Day War against Israel
1973	Faisal halts oil shipments to United States to protest U.S. support of Israel in October War; five-month embargo causes a worldwide oil crisis
1974	OPEC oil-price hikes trigger enormous economic boom in Saudi Arabia
1975	Faisal assassinated in Riyadh by a nephew, Faisal ibn Musa 'id; Faisal's brother, Crown Prince Khalid, becomes king

Index

Rebecca Stefoff holds a Ph.D. in English from the University of Pennsylvania, where she taught from 1974 to 1977. The author of several works of fiction and nonfiction, she currently serves as editorial director of the Chelsea House series PLACES AND PEOPLES OF THE WORLD, to which she has contributed the volume entitled *The West Bank and the Gaza Strip*. She is also the author of *Yasir Arafat* in the Chelsea House series WORLD LEADERS PAST & PRESENT.

Arthur M. Schlesinger, jr., taught history at Harvard for many years and is currently Albert Schweitzer Professor of the Humanities at City University of New York. He is the author of numerous highly praised works in American history and has twice been awarded the Pulitzer Prize. He served in the White House as special assistant to Presidents Kennedy and Johnson.

PICTURE CREDITS

AP/Wide World Photos: pp. 16, 17, 37, 53, 55, 58, 64, 66, 68, 82, 89, 90, 97, 98, 99, 102, 106, 107; Aramco Photo: p. 88; Bettmann Archive: pp. 22, 26–27, 28, 30–31, 38, 41, 44, 49, 70, 71, 73, 93, 103; Freer Gallery of Art, Smithsonian Institution, negative no. 7654B: p. 24; Royal Embassy of Saudi Arabia: p. 14; Donna Sinisgalli: p. 23; United Nations photo: pp. 78, 80; UPI/Bettmann Newsphotos: pp. 2, 12, 15, 18, 19, 20, 29, 32, 34, 42, 46, 48, 50, 52, 56, 57, 59, 60, 62, 69, 72, 77, 81, 84, 85, 86, 92, 94, 95, 96, 100, 104, 105